MW00851941

23

PSYCHIC CRIMINOLOGY

ABOUT THE AUTHORS

WHITNEY S. HIBBARD

Mr. Hibbard has been a criminal justice planner and special program developer (e.g., crime prevention programs, crime-specific interagency teams, career criminal prosecution units, intelligence networks, law enforcement information systems, and corrections facility designs), forensic hypnotist, licensed private investigator, reserve deputy sheriff, martial arts instructor, and senior author of *Forensic Hypnosis: The Practical Application of Hypnosis in Criminal Investigations* (published by Charles C Thomas, Publisher) and *Travel Safely: Don't Be A Target!* Mr. Hibbard is currently working on his doctorate in human science.

RAYMOND W. WORRING

A counseling psychologist and avid student and researcher of parapsychology for four decades, Mr. Worring was director of the Technical Assistance Bureau of the Institute for Social Science Research at the University of Montana, director of the Investigative Research Field Station in Helena, Montana, a licensed private investigator, investigative reporter for CBS News (focusing on unusual phenomena), and special projects developer for the Montana Board of Crime Control. Mr. Worring helped pioneer the field of psychic criminology by actively researching the practical application of psychics in criminal investigations and encouraging their use in law enforcement.

RICHARD BRENNAN

Richard Brennan has been a consulting criminologist, corporate criminal investigator and licensed private investigator. In these capacities he frequently used psychics as investigative aides. Mr. Brennan has been an advisor and columnist for Missing Persons Cyber Center sponsored by Hollywoodnetwork.com. He is a member of the International Narcotics Enforcement Officers Association. Mr. Brennan currently serves as an executive producer for motion picture and television projects and also acts as personal and artistic manager for screenwriters, actors, directors, and producers.

Second Edition

PSYCHIC CRIMINOLOGY

A Guide For Using
Psychics In Investigations

By

WHITNEY S. HIBBARD, M.A.

Criminal Justice Consultant
Past Co-Director, Missoula City/County Crime Attack Team
Past Operations Coordinator, Great Falls/Cascade County Crime Attack Team
Forensic Hypnotist and Instructor
Licensed Private Investigator

RAYMOND W. WORRING, M.A.

Director, Investigative Research Field Station
Past Co-Director, Missoula City/County Crime Attack Team
Past Trainer, Great Falls/Cascade County Crime Attack Team
Forensic Hypnotist and Instructor
Licensed Private Investigator

RICHARD S. BRENNAN

Consulting Criminologist
Former Corporate Criminal Investigator & Licensed Private Investigator
Member, International Narcotics Enforcement Officers Association

Charles C Thomas
PUBLISHER • LTD.
SPRINGFIELD • ILLINOIS • U.S.A.

Published and Distributed Throughout the World by

CHARLES C THOMAS • PUBLISHER, LTD.
2600 South First Street
Springfield, Illinois 62704

This book is protected by copyright. No part of
it may be reproduced in any manner without
written permission from the publisher.

© 2002 by CHARLES C THOMAS • PUBLISHER, LTD.

ISBN 0-398-07288-4 (hard)
ISBN 0-398-07289-2 (paper)

Library of Congress Catalog Card Number: 2002019184

With THOMAS BOOKS *careful attention is given to all details of manufacturing
and design. It is the Publisher's desire to present books that are satisfactory as to their
physical qualities and artistic possibilities and appropriate for their particular use.*
THOMAS BOOKS *will be true to those laws of quality that assure a good name
and good will.*

Printed in the United States of America
RR-R-3

Library of Congress Cataloging-in-Publication Data

Hibbard, Whitney S.
    Psychic criminology: a guide for using psychics in investigations / by
Whitney S. Hibbard, Raymond W. Worring, Richard Brennan. – 2nd ed.
        p. cm.
Includes bibliographical references and index.
ISBN 0-398-07288-4 – ISBN 0-398-07289-2 (pbk.)
1. Parapsychology in criminal investigation–Handbooks, manuals, etc. I.
Worring, Raymond W. II. Brennan, Richard. III. Title.

BF1045.C7 H5 2002
363.2'5–dc21
                                                            2002019184

*For all those investigators and psychics who gave us
their trust and shared their experiences.*

and to

*Ray Worring (1932–1998) without whose inspiration and research
this book would not have been written.*

PREFACE TO SECOND EDITION

Much has happened in the field of psychic criminology since the publication of the first edition of this book twenty years ago, so a second edition is both timely and necessary. Each chapter has been extensively edited and rewritten with much new and significant material added. Sadly, my original co-author, Ray Worring, died in 1998. Without his contribution, it was necessary to bring a new co-author on board, one with considerable experience in the field. That person is Richard Brennan, who contributed by adding sections on *remote viewing* and case histories presented in a new chapter, **PSI CASE FILES**.

The primary purpose of the first edition was to promote the professional use of psychics as an investigative aid in criminal investigations, both criminal and civil. That purpose remains the same. The intent of this book is not to be a critical appraisal; that has been done comprehensively elsewhere, most notably in the highly recommended *The Blue Sense: Psychic Detectives and Crime*, which also is a careful and well-documented look at the many pitfalls of working with psychic sleuths. The first edition was criticized in some quarters for being overly sympathetic and uncritical about the role of psychics in criminal investigations. This criticism has been addressed in this edition by double-checking all our sources and anecdotes, omitting those that are suspect, and adding much new documented material. However, the book remains unapologetically supportive of the use of psychics as investigative aides, as long as they are used in a disciplined, efficient, and professional manner. Persuaded by the scientific evidence from parapsychology, as well as several decades of personal experience in the field, the authors remain convinced of the usefulness of psychic criminology.

Apollo astronaut and consciousness researcher Edgar Mitchell predicted in 1974 that "the production of psi will be understood and harnessed in the same way we presently use electricity and magnetism," and that one future use will be "law enforcement agencies solving crimes and locating missing persons through psychic channels." Although psi has yet to be understood and harnessed, Mitchell's second prediction has come to pass, as we hope to demonstrate in this edition.

W.S.H.

PREFACE

During the past five years the authors have worked intimately with literally dozens of psychics and law enforcement agencies in an effort to examine the feasibility of using psychics as an investigative adjunct. During this period the idea of writing a book on the subject never occurred to us. In fact, many psychics required as a prerequisite to our working with them that we not do so with the motive of publishing. For the most part they also demanded confidentiality. Similarly, all the law enforcement agencies also requested that it not be revealed that they were using psychics. We eventually came to the realization, however, that there was a tremendous need for a comprehensive guide on how to properly use psychics in investigations. We, therefore, have not included any names of psychics (except those already wellknown), law enforcement agencies, or investigators without permission.

All the stories included here are true and, unless otherwise specified, were experienced by us or investigators known to us personally. In a few instances, some minor details have been changed to protect the sources, but the essence remains the same. All the stories were reconstructed from notes or memory, so if there are any errors, the authors request the understanding of the parties directly involved.

For ease of reading and considering that this is not a scholarly text but a practical operations manual, there will be no literary citations. All facts, theories, and studies referred to, however, can be found in the sources listed in the bibliography. A glossary has been included for the reader unfamiliar with parapsychological terminology, and an index is provided for easy reference.

W.S.H.
R.W.W.

ACKNOWLEDGMENTS

The authors wish to acknowledge the following individuals who generously provided assistance and information for this book:

Captain Keith Wolverton (ret.), Cascade County Sheriff's Office
Det. Sgt. Richard Keaton (ret.), Marin County Sheriff's Office
Commander Dennis Miller (ret.), Santa Fe Police Department
Sgt. Dan Chappell (ret.), Santa Fe Police Department
Chief Dennis Nagy (ret.), Carteret Police Department
Detective Bob Lee, Lake Oswego Police Department
Deputy Ferenc Zana, King County Sheriff's Office
Det. Sgt. Fernando Realyvasquez, Pacifica Police Department
Chief Anton Graff, Yorkville Police Department
Sgt. Donald Schwartzkopf, Yorkville Police Department
Roberta Hauser, San Mateo County Sheriff Search & Rescue
Beverly Jaegers, U.S. PSI Squad
Dr. Marcello Truzzi, Psychic Sleuths Project
Gayle Pasternak, for sections from *Tour of Duty: The Diaries of Psychic Bill Ward*
Psychic investigators Annette Martin, Pam Coronado, Laurie McQuary, and Bill Ward
Remote viewers Paul Smith, Lyn Buchanan, and Joe McMoneagle
Gloria de la Cruz, victim's mother
Angel Brennan, for her editorial assistance in Rich Brennan's contributions.
Troy Holter, for his invaluable assistance in editing and proofreading the manuscript.

CONTENTS

PSYCHIC CRIMINOLOGY

Chapter 1

PSYCHIC CRIMINOLOGY: THE STATE OF THE ART

Faced with the ever-mounting problem of crime, law enforcement and criminal justice professionals are examining and using innovative investigative tools. These tools range from the development of sophisticated laboratory techniques in criminalistics, to the use of hypnosis with volunteer victims of and witnesses to crimes, to information obtained from psychics.[1]

In an examination of innovative crime control techniques and investigative procedures conducted from 1978 to 1980, involving thousands of miles of travel throughout the western United States and Canada, visiting dozens of law enforcement and criminal justice agencies, the authors (WH & RW)[2] found that most agencies have used the services of psychics as an adjunct to traditional investigative procedures. More recently this experience has been confirmed by the new co-author, consulting criminologist Richard Brennan.

The initial contact with a psychic commonly takes the form of a psychic calling the local police department or sheriff's office with information on a current serious case. The well-intentioned psychic usually does not have a personal contact within the department and ends up talking to an unsympathetic detective. The resulting encounter often proves to be awkward for both. In the first place, it is not easy for a psychic to approach the authorities for fear of being thought a crackpot—or even a suspect—if the information proves accurate. After all, up to 1951, mediums in England were legally classed as

---

[1] The reader is referred to Chapter 3 and the Glossary for definitions and explanations of unusual, new, or technical terms.

[2] Only where necessary for clarification will the specific authors be designated.

3

"rogues and vagabonds" and were subject to prosecution. On the other side, law enforcement officers–often skeptical by nature and suspicious by training–are similarly hesitant when approached by psychics, because they usually (a) do not know with whom they are dealing, (b) do not believe in psychic abilities, (c) believe that they do not need the help of psychics, or (d) won't want to commit resources to follow up information that may not be substantive. Even if the investigator is predisposed to accepting psychically obtained information as worth a follow-up investigation, he or she may have difficulty justifying the necessary man-hours to superiors. Then, of course, there is always the fear of adverse publicity. According to Captain Charles Hensley (ret.) of the Billings, Montana, Police Department, many law enforcement agencies consult with psychics but "most do not admit it because if the public or press found out, they'd think we were nuts."

Many law enforcement agencies first encounter the realm of the psychic when they have exhausted all leads and investigative techniques on a major case that has the public's attention. As a last resort the department, usually through the suggestion of an interested detective, will take the initiative and approach a psychic, whether a famous one who is in the media or a local person known to someone in the department. This is exactly what happened to Capt. Keith Wolverton (ret.) twenty-seven years ago when he contacted Harold Sherman, a famous psychic and author, on a dead-end case. Wolverton was sufficently impressed that "From that time on, I have contributed much of my time working with psychics, attempting to develop an understanding of how they work and how to utilize their information in my investigations" (Wolverton's story is related in Chapter 6: PSI CASE FILES).

In other situations a law enforcement agency may be compelled to cooperate with a psychic. For example, the family of a crime victim or missing person may contact a well-known psychic and even pay for an on-site psychic reading or investigation. This is precisely what happened in the John Wayne Gacy serial murder case in Illinois. The family of one of the victims requested that the police department bring in nationally known psychic detective Dorothy Allison (now deceased) to work on the case at the family's expense.

It is also not unknown for a psychic to march into a detective's office to offer intimate and accurate details of some unsolved case, thus launching a long-term working relationship. This happened to

Det. Sgt. Richard Keaton of the Marin County Sheriff's Office. One day a total stranger visited him in his office, introduced herself as Annette Martin (profiled in Chapter 2 and Chapter 6), and proceeded to describe minute details of an unsolved crime that only Keaton was privy to. This began a several decades professional relationship of working on criminal cases.

Whatever form the contact with psychics first takes, it is too often a frustrating experience for both officer and psychic. This is because the officer generally does not know how to deal with the psychic because there is no departmental program or guidelines for their use. Similarly, the psychic does not generally know how to deal with law enforcement personnel and often is frustrated in the attempt. All too frequently, the initial encounter is the first and last between a skeptical officer and an untested psychic. If the information obtained proves incorrect, the officer may self-justifiably exclaim that he or she knew it wouldn't work anyway. Or, if the information proves correct, the officer may dismissively consider it a coincidence or a lucky guess.

There are yet law enforcement agencies whose exposure to the paranormal comes through one of their own sworn personnel. Most departments have one particular officer whose intuition, hunches, and gut feelings seem to be uncannily accurate, whether it's the patrol officer who always seems to be in the right place at the right time or the detective whose hunches prove consistently accurate. For example, one Montana policeman averages two burglaries in progress per year, whereas the national average is one per career per officer. One evening in Missoula, Montana, a detective on patrol casually remarked that he felt that the Super America on Orange Street was going to be hit that night–a risky prediction, considering the low incidence of robberies in this small western town. A half hour later it was robbed! Other officers occasionally have staked out buildings or followed vehicles on gut feelings to be proven correct by foiling criminal activity in progress.

In another incident in Montana, a police officer on night shift told his partner about a dream he had the night before in which he responded to a disturbance call involving weapons in a particular area of town. Once in the house (in the dream), the officer walked down the stairs to the basement, whereupon he woke up. Later that night the officer and his partner were dispatched to a disturbance involving weapons in the area of town indicated in the dream. The officer followed his partner down the stairs to the basement when his partner's riot gun accidentally discharged, hitting the officer in the head and killing him instantly. It was discovered later that the dead officer's wife had urged him not to go on patrol that night, because she felt that something bad was going to happen. She also said that her husband had not wanted to go to work either and had kissed her goodbye as if for the last time. Another patrol officer on the same shift later said that he had had a strong gut feeling that same day, for no discernible reason, that it would be a bad night.

An investigator for a rural fire department was at the scene of a motorcycle accident in which the cyclist's neck was broken. The investigator was holding the victim's head steady until the ambulance arrived. As he was doing so, he felt a hand on his shoulder. He turned his head around to see who was there and to his surprise no one was there. He shrugged it off and went back to applying a steady tension on the victims's neck. He then felt a tapping on his shoulder. He turned, and again no one was there. Feeling uneasy, he looked up behind him and saw a misty shape, and it struck him that it was the victim's "spirit". The victim died shortly thereafter in the hospital.

The same investigator was applying CPR to an older woman. He definitely heard her say, even though she was DOA, "Please stop." He had the distinct impression that she was trying to tell him to stop because she wanted to die. He continued CPR only to again hear her say, "Please stop." This so startled him that he stopped.

An off-duty Great Falls, Montana, city police officer was sitting with a friend in a mobile home in a large trailer court. Suddenly he saw or sensed–he wasn't quite sure which–two "spirits" fly past him, although he had never experienced anything of this nature before. He dismissed the event until he learned the next day that there was a homicide-suicide at the same time of his experience at the far end of that trailer court.

Over an eight-year period (1975–1983) the authors (WH and RW) were involved intimately with law enforcement and criminal justice personnel in the capacity of developing and implementing special innovative crime control programs. During this period, we spent a great deal of our own time examining the feasibility and effectiveness of using psychics as an investigative aid. Considerable time and effort went into identifying and recruiting potential psychics, testing their abilities, developing techniques of psychic investigation, following up leads obtained, and evaluating their effectiveness. We were sufficiently impressed with our experiences to encourage the further use and testing of psychics in investigation and to outline some general procedures for their use. It is the purpose of this book to serve as a basic guide to be used by any interested law enforcement or criminal justice agency or individual investigator who wishes to use psychics in investigations, whether criminal or civil. When recruited, tested, and used properly, psychics have proven to be of substantial value to investigators. The authors' experience supports the research of Dr. Richard Broughton, a prominent parapsychologist and research director of the Institute for Parapsychology in Durham, North Carolina:

> There is already a collection of cases in which a psychic *has* definitely helped investigations. Psychics have led police to bodies or have described locations so accurately that police could find them. Psychics have saved precious time in locating lost children and uncovered vital clues in criminal investigations. In a few cases psychics were able to describe a suspect or lead police to him, whereupon traditional methods completed the investigation. For many of these cases sworn law officers have stated that the case *would not have been solved without the psychic's help.*

When psychics are used incorrectly, however, the results are usually disappointing. It is the authors' belief that properly tested psychics should be used as an ongoing volunteer resource and not only as a last resort (which is too often the case). It is the intent of this book to provide interested parties with the background understanding and procedures necessary to establish a viable and effective working relationship with reputable psychics. This book should be of value both to the reader who has had experience with psychics or has yet to work with one.

That the time is ripe for such a comprehensive guide for using psychics in criminal investigations is evidenced by:

1. The high level of interest encountered by the authors around the country.
2. The increasing use by law enforcement officers and victims' families of established psychic sleuths (like Annette Martin, Nancy Czetli, Bill Ward, and Philip Jordon), and use of groups of psychics, such as the U.S. PSI Squad.
3. The recent interest in *remote viewing*, which has been developed by the U.S. government.

4. The formation of nonprofit groups and organizations composed of former law enforcement personnel and psychics dedicated to promoting the use of psychics in investigation.
5. The appearance of numerous television specials and popular books on psychic crime detection.
6. The teaching of seminars to law enforcement personnel on how to develop their own ESP skills.
7. The conducting of several studies on the effectiveness of psychics in major crime investigations, including two by the Los Angeles Police Department.
8. The publication of several articles on the subject in professional law enforcement journals and criminal justice texts.
9. The founding of the Psychic Sleuths Project in 1980, whose purpose is to serve as an international clearinghouse for data on the use of psychics by police (which as of this writing has data on 350 psychics who have worked with law enforcement agencies and victims' families).[3]

In addition, the general public also seems to be more sympathetic toward the use of psychics by law enforcement agencies, although most agencies opt to keep their work in this area strictly confidential. According to Chief James Basil of the Buckland, Massachusetts Police Department, one of the few police officials to go public on this subject, "A lot of police departments may use psychics, but they will only admit it off the record." Similary, Chief Anton Graff of the Yorkville, Illinois Police Department says that after he went public with his successful work with a psychic, he was receiving between forty and fifty inquires per year from law enforcement officers from all over the country. "Most were off the record, saying 'Hey Chief, ya know my department can't know that I'm calling, but. . . .'" In all likelihood, increasing public pressure eventually will force law enforcement personnel to use psychics more frequently. This is evidenced by the escalating number of requests for help that psychics receive from victims' families.

---

[3] The authors highly encourage law enforcement officers and the psychics who work with them to contact the Psychic Sleuths Project to share their stories, both successes and failures, which will help build its data bank and sharing of information. Write Dr. Marcello Truzzi, Psychic Sleuths Project, Center for Scientific Anomalies Research, 5010 Willis Road, Grass Lake, MI 49240, or telephone at (517) 522-3551.

The current situation is summed up nicely by Karen Henrikson and Chief Kozenczak (ret.), chief investigator on the John Wayne Gacy case, in their article "Still Beyond Belief: The Use of Psychics in Homicide Investigations": "The world of parapsychology has a great deal to offer. . . . Having once experienced the positive attributes a psychic can lend to a case, parapsychology seems to be a natural companion to the world of criminology."

One of the purposes of this book is to foster that companionship.

Chapter 2

A SHORT HISTORY OF PSYCHIC CRIMINOLOGY

Throughout the ages humans have sought to divine the answers and solutions to many questions and problems, including the determination of the source of ill fortune and ill will, the whereabouts of lost objects and people, and the perpetrators of crimes. Continuing to this day, men and women of all races and nationalities have consulted various oracles to look into the future, examined the stars and planets to determine the forces that influence their lives, and visited seers, shamans, witch doctors, and practitioners of the occult arts for information and advice.

One would naturally assume that in the arena of law enforcement and criminal justice–one of the most conservative and pragmatic of professions–that any involvement in such fringe areas would be shunned. On the whole this has been true, but there have been many notable exceptions. Probably the first officially recorded instance of psychic crime solving was in France in 1692, when the King's procurator enlisted the services of a dowser, who successfully solved the sensational meat cleaver murder of a wine merchant and his wife.

In recent times, innovative departments and desperate detectives have used psychics as an investigative tool. In examining the literature on psychic criminology, we find no fewer than a dozen books detailing the stories of "psychic sleuths," "psychic investigators," and "psychic detectives,"[1] as they are commonly called. An example is Peter

---

[1] This is a misnomer as no psychic should be considered a detective (unless the psychic is a sworn officer) but an informant, and any information provided should be treated accordingly, i.e., as hearsay. Furthermore, psychics do not solve cases, the police do, although psychics may be of considerable assistance.

Hurkos, the famous Dutch psychic, whose alleged clairvoyant abilities began at the age of thirty in 1941 as a result of falling thirty feet onto his head. When he regained consciousness four days later, he claimed that he was privy to peoples' subconscious thoughts, desires, and motives; in other words, he could see clairvoyantly. This began his long career of aiding the police in many countries on cases of arson, murder, theft, and other crimes. There is the example of Gerard Croiset, another famous contemporary Dutch psychic, who aided police and families of victims in dozens of cases. He was reputed to be particularly adept at finding missing people and solving murder cases and was studied at length (albeit somewhat dubiously) by Professor W. H. C. Tenhaeff, director of the Parapsychological Institute of the University of Utrecht, Holland. Another contemporary Dutch psychic, Marinus Dykshoorn, claimed to have proven his abilities to such an extent that the Dutch government licensed him as a "practitioner of the psychic arts," and the passport office recognized his psychic status by labeling his occupation in his passport as "clairvoyant." Dykshoorn credited himself with solving some difficult cases, locating lost graves, accurately foretelling events, and even tracking a thief by telephone in a distant country.

Unfortunately, with most of these high-profile psychic sleuths, it is difficult to sort out fact from fiction, reality from self-promotion, truth from misrepresentation, and authentic from unsubstantiated claims. Unquestionably, there is a common tendency of psychic sleuths to take credit where little is due. In the words of Dr. Truzzi and Arthur Lyons, authors of *The Blue Sense: Psychic Detectives and Crime*, the popular accounts of these sleuths "are offered without substantiation; some are distortions of fact, while others are flatly untrue. In virtually all of them, the psychics' many documentable failures are blatantly ignored." Yet, Truzzi and Lyons conclude that "Discounting fabrications and confabulations by psychics and their biographers, media distortions, and cases of outright fraud, there remains a considerable body of documented cases in which psychic sleuths have scored impressive and seemingly inexplicable successes. . . . The case for the blue sense [i.e., psychic ability] may not be totally convincing, but it is far more substantial than many critics have presumed."

One such success story is that of another famous European psychic investigator, the Hungarian clairvoyant, Janos Kele, whose record seems to stand up under scrutiny. Kele's abilities were tested successfully by Dr. Karlis Osis of Duke University's parapsychology laboratory and by Professor Hans Driesch of Leipzig University, who called him a "classic clairvoyant." It has been claimed that hundreds of people owe their lives to him. A deputy police chief in Budapest, who used Kele in his missing persons bureau, stated that Kele averaged an 80 percent accuracy rate and that on some days he was 100 percent accurate. In one typical case, the police were informed on December 28, 1935, by a distraught woman that her niece had run away, leaving a suicide note. Kele said that the girl had gone to one specific bridge on the Danube intending to jump off, but changed her mind. He cautioned, though, that she might throw herself under a train. Patrol officers were sent out, and she was found at a train station. Kele died in 1957 without ever accepting fees or rewards and was virtually unknown outside of Hungary, because he sought no publicity, unlike Hurkos, Croiset, and Dykshoorn.

Yet another famous European psychic is Vanga Dimitrova, a blind Hungarian clairvoyant. On the basis of an impressive track record of finding missing persons, naming killers, and other paranormal crime-detection feats, she was tested by Dr. Lozanov and a special government commission of examiners, who both proclaimed her genuine. She became a state-employed psychic in 1966.

In the United States there are many notable psychic sleuths, such as Irene F. Hughes from Chicago, who is reported to have helped solve several murder cases for the Illinois police. In one homicide case she allegedly provided police with the name and address of the murderer. In another case, Mrs. Hughes reportedly told a police chief that a man being held on suspicion of murder was responsible for four other homicides. The chief assigned her to work with one of his sergeants and over the next six months she provided information that helped lead to the four bodies. In one case in which the authors are personally familiar, she was hired by the family to do a psychic reading on a suspected murder case (she does not charge when consulted directly by law enforcement). Mrs. Hughes called the sheriff of the sparsely populated county in Montana from Chicago at a prearranged time. She wanted only to know the bare facts, such as the victim's name and location of the crime, making it clear that she did not want any unsolicited information, such as the sheriff's reconstruction of the crime. The sheriff, at first skeptical, quickly became a believer when Hughes started telling him personal things about his own life, "Things my own wife doesn't know," he said. When the reading was received in the mail, it was a virtual reconstruction of the crime. Specifically, Hughes correctly stated that, based on the victim's astrological chart, the killer was a woman from the victim's own home who shot him suddenly in self-defense after she instigated an argument, that it occurred a long distance from home in a public place near a stream, that another woman was on the scene and witnessed the event, that there had been marital problems and concerns over money, and that no hard evidence would be turned up to indicate murder.

Beverly Jaegers (recently deceased) of Sappington, Missouri, founded the U.S. PSI Squad in 1971–a group of trained and experienced *remote viewers* (as she prefers to call them)–to work on cases throughout the country (several hundred as of this writing). Jaegers became a licensed private investigator in 1974 and was an independent journalist by profession. The daughter of a policeman, Jaegers took a logical, analytical, controlled approach to her case work, using *remote viewing* as her primary modality. Jaegers' U.S. PSI Squad, a private detective agency registered with the State of Missouri, receives numerous requests from law enforcement for their assistance (for whom they work confidentially and *pro bono,* because they regard their work a public service). The author of two books, *Psychometry, The Science of Touch* and *The Psychic Paradigm,* Jaegers has been the subject of newspaper reports and television specials, has taught a course in psychometry at the St. Louis University City School of Continuing Education, and has trained police officers in remote viewing.

And then there's Dorothy Allison, a Nutley, New Jersey, housewife whose services have been used by hundreds of distraught families and numerous police and sheriff's departments since 1967. With mixed results, she has consulted on such high-profile cases as the Son of Sam, John Wayne Gacy, and Wayne Williams serial murder cases. According to Chief Robert DeLitta of the Nutley Police Department, "There's many police out there that have used her successfully and really think that she does have the ability to come across with valid information. . . . The number of agencies that use her a second and third time are numerous."

A psychic detective of special note is deputy sheriff Philip Jordon from the Tioga County Sheriff's Office in New York State who, according to a report in *The National Law Journal,* has worked on murders in thirty-seven states. James Coons of the Addison County,

Vermont, Sheriff's Office, who has used Deputy Jordan's services, says that "He's located a lot of missing persons. His big thing is bodies. He has a documented track record that's very credible. We might be able to use him as a contributing factor to probable cause as a basis for a search warrant."

When Noreen Renier first lectured at the FBI Academy in Quantico, Virginia, in 1981, her work with police was considered controversial. As of this writing, she is a well-known psychic investigator who claims to have worked on several hundred cases with city, county, and state law enforcement agencies in thirty-eight states and five foreign countries. Ms. Renier has also lectured at The Second International Seminar on Advancing the Scientific Investigation of Crimes in Durham, England; the Sarasota Police Department in Florida; the St. Louis (Missouri) County & Municipal Police Academy; the Law Enforcement & Corrections Third International Conference in Miami; the Central Florida Criminal Justice Institute in Orlando; and the Virginia Bureau of Forensic Science in Richmond, to name a few. Ms. Renier also has appeared on such television shows as "America's Most Wanted" and "Unsolved Mysteries." In the authors experience, Renier was difficult to contact, reluctant to correspond or share any case material for this book, and charges a large fee for her services.

Some of the exploits of Bill Ward, a retired printer and psychic investigator from Lockport, Illinois, are chronicled in Gayle Pasternak's compelling biography, *Tour of Duty*. Ward, a decorated Vietnam veteran, was recently featured in the ABC special, *Psychic Detectives*. Police detectives have used Ward at various stages of their investigations since 1971. An article in *Law and Order* magazine (September, 1986) earned him national recognition as a credible psychic and valuable investigative aide. To date, he has worked on approximately 400 homicide cases. Ward says, "I get pictures–faces, scenes, areas–just like when you turn on the TV." Speaking from extensive personal experience with Ward, Chief Anton Graff of the Yorkville, Illinois, Police Department says that "Bill has the amazing ability to give a full description of a crime."

Nancy Myer is a well-known psychic investigator from Greensburg, Pennsylvania. Articles about her have appeared in many publications, including popular magazines and books. Her national television appearances include "Unsolved Mysteries," "The Other Side," "48

Hours," and "*Geraldo.*" The most comprehensive description of her early work is contained in her autobiography, *Silent Witness: The True Story of a Psychic Detective.* Ms. Myer lectures, teaches meditation, and consults with police departments nationwide, as well as privately with individuals.

A New Jersey mother of three and wife of a newspaper editor, Nancy Czetli has worked on several hundred police investigations in twenty states for such law enforcement agencies as the Delaware State Police and Winchester, Virginia, Sheriff's Office. She has appeared on numerous television and radio shows.

We also have Pam Coronado, who has been involved in psychic criminal work since 1996 when a dream provided her with the information needed to help a search party locate a missing woman in California. Since then, she has been involved actively in helping solve local and regional crimes and mysteries, such as missing persons cases. She has consulted in this capacity with local, state, federal, international, and private agencies. Ms. Coronado uses clairvoyance and psychometry to gain insight into a crime or missing person's case. By holding a personal possession of the victim, she can "tune in" to the victim and learn of his or her current state and clues about their location. Although no psychic can be 100 percent accurate or provide all the answers, Ms. Coronado's work has proven to be astonishingly accurate and helpful on numerous occasions. Ms. Coronado currently holds her own private investigator license and lives in Oxnard, California.

Although not as well known as some other psychic sleuths, Annette Martin of Campbell, California, is one of the best. The reason for her low profile is that until recently she kept her several decades of psychic investigation work quiet. For instance, Det. Sgt. Richard Keaton (ret.), a thirty-five year veteran of the Marin County Sheriff's Office, worked extensively with Martin since 1975 "not only because she was so good, but because she wasn't a publicity hound, and could be trusted with details of the investigation." Martin has worked on many major cases for numerous police departments, sheriff's offices, the U.S. Coast Guard, the San Francisco District Attorney's Office, and the FBI, often with impressive results. Martin's work has been featured recently on "48 Hours," "Lifetime," and a BBC special *Extra Sensory Perception.* In 1999 Martin and Keaton teamed up to start a business, A Case Closed, to consult on criminal cases for law enforcement agencies on a fee basis.

Numerous other well-known psychic sleuths could be profiled–such as Ron Nolan, Dixie Yeterian, Judy Belle, and Laurie McQuary–but our purpose has been served of introducing the reader to a few of these people (some of their success stories are told in (Chapter 6, PSI CASE FILES).

A significant development since the first edition of this book is the U.S. government-sponsored psi research, especially in the area of extrasensory intelligence gathering by means of a technique called *remote viewing*, or RV (see Chapter 3 for an overview). With the decommissioning of the government's program in 1995, the highly trained remote viewers were free to become involved in the private sector. Prominent remote viewers during the government program were Joseph McMoneagle, Leonard "Lyn" Buchanan, and Paul H. Smith. All three of these government-trained viewers currently have ongoing programs involving consulting, research, teaching, writing, and lecturing and lend their services to law enforcement agencies.

Joe McMoneagle, originally assigned as a military intelligence officer, spent seventeen years with the government's RV program. He worked for fourteen years as a consultant for remote viewing with Stanford Research Institute (SRI), then for Science Applications International Corporation, and is a Research Associate for Cognitive Science Laboratory of Palo Alto, California. In addition, McMoneagle is the Director for Anomalous Cognition Development at the Laboratory of Fundamental Research in Palo Alto. He is also co-founder of the Intuitive Studies Institute, a newly formed nonprofit organization that promotes and supports future paranormal research. Having participated in more than 4,000 remote viewings under laboratory conditions, McMoneagle is the only remote viewer to have performed under laboratory controls while being filmed by major television networks. McMoneagle was awarded the Legion of Merit, one of the Army's highest peacetime awards for "producing crucial and vital intelligence unavailable from any other source" for such agencies as the Defense Intelligence Agency, CIA, DEA, the Secret Service, and even the Joint Chiefs of Staff. McMoneagle also has worked as a remote viewer for numerous police departments, a number of State's Attorneys General Offices, the FBI, U.S. Customs, Department of Defense, and the National Security Council. In correspondence with this author (RB), McMoneagle explained that he cannot provide information on specific cases or clients because of his guarantee of total confidentiality. McMoneagle is the owner of Intuitive Intelligence Applications, Inc. in Nellysford, Virginia, and is the author of several books.

Leonard "Lyn" Buchanan was a remote viewer in the government's program for nearly nine years. He has trained military and government remote viewers and now trains remote viewers in the private sector. Presently, Buchanan is executive director of Problems> Solutions>Innovations (PSI) in Almagordo, New Mexico. PSI was originally a data-analysis company, but when the CIA declassified its RV program, a demand arose for RV services and training in the private sector. So, PSI now spends more than 90 percent of its time involved in RV work. A continuing public service, which is sponsored solely by Buchanan, and which uses the volunteer services of other remote viewers and his own students, is the Assigned Witness Program (AWP), currently directed by Deputy Ferenc Zana of the King County Sheriff's Office. The AWP performs free RV services for police and other public-sponsored investigative agencies. According to Buchanan, AWP guarantees complete anonymity to the departments for which they work. "Also, it is our strict policy to never contact a law enforcement agency to offer our services. We work for those who call us, and if the work we do is of sufficient quality, they will tell other investigators and we will be called again. We do not want publicity or even credit for our participation. We only want feedback."

Paul H. Smith served in the government's RV program from 1983 to 1990. Smith was the primary author for the government's RV program training manual and served as theory instructor for new trainees, as well as recruiting officer and unit security officer. He is credited with more than 1,000 training and operational RV sessions. Smith was commissioned as a military intelligence officer. His military assignments included Arabic linguist, electronic warfare operator, strategic intelligence officer for a special operations unit, Mid-East desk officer, tactical intelligence officer with the 101st Airborne Division during Desert Storm/Shield, strategic intelligence officer in the Collection Directorate of the Defense Intelligence Agency, and chief of the Intelligence and Security Division for the Military District of Washington, D.C., from which he retired in 1996. He and his work as a remote viewer have been featured in national television programs. He works as a freelance remote viewer and RV consultant, owns and operates Remote Viewing Instructional Services, Inc. in Round Rock, Texas, a company offering remote viewing training courses to individuals. Smith's new book, *Reading the Enemy's Mind,* is an historical overview of remote viewing.

The increase in the quality and number of psychic investigators (including the recent entrance of remote viewers) who are involved actively in working with law enforcement in the United States is an indication of the interest in and acceptance of the psychic's evolving role in criminal investigation. Some psychic investigators have built credible track records by helping solve major cases. We will cover some actual cases in Chapter 6, PSI CASE FILES.

In addition to the repeated use of the psychic talent of well-known and experienced psychics, investigators are sometimes aided by the spontaneous and isolated paranormal experiences of otherwise nonpsychic individuals. In such instances there is generally a strong or close personal tie between the psychic "receiver" and the "sender," usually a blood relationship, intimate friend, or lover. In one instance a young woman, who never had any paranormal experiences before, had a distinct feeling that her fiance was about to commit suicide. Succumbing to her persistent demands, an ambulance crew took her to where she felt him to be. En route she exclaimed that he had fired his gun but was still alive. They found him exactly where she led them, shot in the chest, although still alive. Similarly, there are literally dozens of well-documented instances of mothers and wives feeling, seeing, or somehow knowing the instant of their son's or husband's death in war.

In not all instances of spontaneous and isolated paranormal experiences are there emotional or blood bonds. In one reported case a housewife, in response to an irresistible urge, spontaneously began to write "automatically," even though she had never been interested in the paranormal. The source of the automatic writing identified itself by name as the victim of a recent well-publicized murder. The "spirit's" communication gave a detailed physical description, the occupation, partial name, and complete address of the murderer, all of which proved correct.

It is not unusual that the success stories of psychics in investigations are reported and remembered, whereas the failures are ignored and forgotten; it is only the successes that are newsworthy and hence get the publicity. It must be remembered, however, that even the best psychic sleuths have mostly failures and only partial successes. The investigator embarking on the use of psychics as an investigative aid is forewarned that psychic solutions to cases are rare. Actual convictions in criminal cases using psychics are rarer still. An exception is the case of Rosemarie Kerr, a Cypress, California ordained minister, whose specific information led directly to the arrest and conviction of two murder suspects 2,000 miles away in Louisiana. District Attorney W. J. LeBlanc exclaimed that "there was absolutely no way that it could have been by chance. This woman is a genuine psychic. She's the real thing." But just as the best interrogator does not get a confession out of every guilty suspect interrogated, or the best detective solve every case investigated, the best psychic should not be expected to provide useful information on every case. On the other hand, to deny the possibility and reality of the occasional success stories is shortsighted and unrealistic in the face of the evidence and the cumulative experience of scores of investigators. Furthermore, the authors' own considerable experience with using psychics in investigations has persuaded us that they can be a useful and worthwhile investigative adjunct. A reasoned approach, we advocate, is that expressed by Capt. Wolverton (ret.): "In the past 27 years, I have worked with dozens of psychics on dozens of major cases, and even in the absence of actually solving a case, remain convinced of the value of pursuing this mode of investigation." Similarly, Dr. Gary Kaufman, a forensic psychologist with the Michigan State Police, says that "While it is an investigative tool with a low probability of success, if there is nothing else to go on we will try it."

Additionally, the authors' ethnographic study of the use of psychics by law enforcement personnel has impressed us with the extent to which they have been used by departments of all sizes and localities. In the several dozen law enforcement agencies we have personal experience with, there is not a single one that has not had some sort of experience with psychics. Of course their degree of experience ranges from a single call from an alleged psychic to the ongoing use of several well-tested ones. This personal finding virtually invalidates a 1975 survey of the use of psychics by police in which 100 questionnaires were sent to the largest city police departments in the country. Sixty-eight departments responded and, not surprisingly, only seven admitted that they had used psychics. All seven departments claimed that the psychic information was of no help in solving the cases (as will be seen later, this is also not surprising). A similar 1993 questionnaire survey of the fifty largest cities in the United States found that 65 percent "do not use and have never used psychics." For obvious reasons, a mail questionnaire from an impersonal source is not a good way to get an accurate assessment on the use of psychics in law enforcement. After all, what self-respecting department would voluntarily open itself to criticism by using such an unorthodox and unscientific procedure? Out of a fear of negative publicity most departments will not admit that they have ever used psychics. Even those who do use psychics frequently only do so on an unofficial basis, meaning that as far as anyone else is concerned, they aren't used. (For example, "officially" the FBI does not use psychics,[2] yet, based on the author's and others personal experience, "unofficially" they do. Furthermore, the person completing the questionnaire may honestly believe that his or her department has not used psychics, when the truth of the matter is that he or she simply does not know. An accurate assessment of the use of psychics by law enforcement, then, can only be obtained through personal contact, and then only when that contact is by someone perceived and trusted as a professional colleague. Being in this position of trust, the authors have learned the actual state of affairs in many departments that no questionnaire would ever reveal. For instance, a sheriff's department in a remote western county known as a "John Birch stronghold" took the initiative and contacted a nationally known psychic on several cases; no outsider, however, will ever know this. And a detective from a small police department, unbeknownst to anyone in his department, sent some cases to a famous psychic.

In recent years the subject of psychic criminology has gained more professional interest and acceptance. Professional law enforcement and criminal justice publications, and even a criminology textbook, have published serious articles examining the subject, including *Policing, Police Chief, The National Law Review, Practical Homicide Investigation,* and *Journal of Police Science and Administration.* Several law enforcement agencies have instituted policies regulating their use of psychics, and several graduate theses on the subject have been writ-

---

[2] According to a 1993 statement by FBI spokesperson Kelley Cibulas, "The FBI does not hire psychics and does not plan to hire psychics to work on investigation. However, psychics, just as any other U.S. citizen, will offer information on cases and investigators will assess information they give just as they would information given by anyone else."

ten. A few law enforcement agencies have sponsored lectures and seminars on psychic criminology, and some officers have attended seminars to enhance their own intuitive abilities. Psychics have even lectured at the FBI Academy. A report by the California Department of Justice on the police use of psychics concluded that "a talented psychic can assist you by helping to locate a geographic area of a missing person, narrow the number of leads to be concentrated upon, highlight information that has been overlooked, or provide information previously unknown to the investigator." And the prestigious law enforcement magazine *Police Chief* concluded that, despite certain concerns, "individuals with bona fide psychic ability offer a unique and potentially valuable investigative skill."

The field of psychic criminology also has witnessed the formation of many groups–some still operational, some now defunct–dedicated to the practical application of psychics in investigations, including the U.S. PSI Squad in Missouri (mentioned earlier), the North Texas Parapsychology Association, the Professional Psychics United Psychic Rescue Team in Illinois, the Society for Psychic Investigation in Arizona, the Mobius Group in California, the Canadian Society of Questors, the Canadian Psychic Systems Research Group, the Investigative Research Field Station in Montana, the United Sensitives of America in California, PsiCom in California, and the San Diego Sheriff's Psychic Reserve.

A word of encouragement is due to those investigators who are courageous and open-minded enough to use psychics as investigative aids. In so doing they risk criticism from the public, press, and peers, jeopardize their careers, and invite ostracism by their professional colleagues. As pioneers they follow a lonely road, not waiting for science to provide a plausible explanation for the paranormal. Predictably, when scientific corroboration eventually happens, paranormal abilities will be demystified, and we will witness a surge in the use of psychics in many quarters. Just as graphology and hypnosis were once considered superstitious nonsense, both are now accepted as valid scientific tools and are used by law enforcement as investigative tools. We believe the same holds true for psychic abilities. In conclusion, we may look to the prophetic words of Sir Arthur Conan Doyle, an ardent spiritualist and creator of Sherlock Holmes, who in 1925 predicted that the detectives of the future would be, or at least employ, clairvoyants and mediums.

Chapter 3

THE PSYCHIC, PARANORMAL ABILITIES, SCIENTIFIC EVIDENCE, AND THEORY

Before discussing the procedures for identifying, recruiting, testing, and using psychics in the next chapter, it is necessary to review what is meant by "psychic," who is psychic, what the prevalent (and relevant) psychic abilities are, scientific evidence for their existence, and a possible theoretical explanation. In the modern world hardly a week goes by without hearing or seeing some reference to the psychic, whether it be the latest psychic predictions headlined in the tabloids or a psychic thriller on television or in films, or a news magazine featuring a psychic detective, yet few people give any serious deliberation to the validity of psychic abilities. This is not surprising, because we live in a culture in which the prevailing scientific and religious dogmas are at best dismissive of, or at worst hostile to, anything paranormal.

For the purposes of this book a "psychic" may be defined or described as *any person who receives information by means other than the five senses.* Such means may include telepathically receiving thoughts and impressions, seeing events extrasensorily at a distance, and gaining information by holding an object, to name a few. "Psychic" is also used to refer to intuitive persons and abilities in general and is often used synonymously with "sensitive" and "intuitive." The latter terms are often preferred, because they lack some of the negative connotations of "psychic."

It is unfortunate that this culture tends to stigmatize those who claim to be psychic as eccentric, strange, or even crazy, because most anyone has intuitive abilities. The authors have sought out more than a 100 psychics throughout the country and, although we have met a few "space cadets," many of the most talented have been normal middle-class Americans, including businessmen, housewives, a mechanic, an aerospace engineer, a medical doctor, a college professor, a psychologist, military personnel, and even law enforcement officers and a former police commissioner. Demographically, researcher Stephan Schwartz has found that psychic investigators "are middle-aged and middle class. Often traditional in style, they come across as professionals who take what they do very seriously and value their partnerships with the police." Similarly, Truzzi and Lyons "found most professional psychics sincere and concerned individuals anxious to help others."

This is not to discount the fact that there are those who promote themselves as professional psychics who are actually publicity-seeking pseudo-psychics. We do not mean to discount the possibility that there are phony psychic sleuths looking for gullible clients to bilk. This ever-present possibility, however, is largely circumvented by the procedures outlined herein; that is, using predominantly local, tested psychics on a confidential basis for no fee. It's not that professional psychics should not charge a reasonable fee for their services; it simply seems that there is a positive correlation between a concern with money and the pseudo-psychic. Furthermore, most psychics, even professional psychic investigators, work for law enforcement for free.

Most psychics and parapsychologists believe that psychic abilities of various sorts are innate in most people and can be developed to differing degrees through proper training. For yet unknown reasons some people seem to be born with specific psychic abilities, whereas others may develop psychic skills of one sort or another later in life. Dr. Edgar Mitchell, the Apollo 14 astronaut who turned his attention from the exploration of outer space to inner space after walking on the moon, states that the evidence suggests that psychic abilities are "quite natural and likely common in humans, though latent and seldom manifest. . . . We [are] possibly seeing the emergence of an evolutionary attribute, or the residue from an earlier one that [is] now fading." Dr. Richard Broughton believes that "we simply do not know if psychic ability is something everyone has, but we do know that psychic experiences are widespread. . . . In some cases people acquire information in ways that, on the surface, seem to go beyond any of the conventional communication pathways that biology and psychology have identified."

The psychic abilities that some people manifest are multiple and varied. The most common, and the ones of importance to the investigator, are listed and defined below.

Extrasensory Perception (ESP) is the reception of information by means other than the usual physical senses and without using logical inference. ESP (also referred to as *psi*) is a blanket term covering most psychic abilities but is generally divided into the specific abilities of telepathy, clairvoyance, and precognition. The term was first coined by Dr. J. B. Rhine of the Duke University Parapsychology Laboratory in 1934.

Telepathy is the ability to communicate directly with another person's mind extrasensorily. This generally takes the form of a direct intuitive experience of another person's mental state or thoughts. Investigatively, this ability is used primarily by a psychic to obtain information from the perpetrator of a crime as to his or her state of mind, thoughts, motives, and truth or falsity of alibis. Some psychic investigators claim to telepathically communicate with the spirits of deceased victims of violent crimes.

Clairvoyance is the ability to acquire information extrasensorily at a distance. (*Clairvoyance* is a French term meaning "clear seeing," and although some consider it synonymous with *remote viewing*, we will treat the latter separately.) A specific form of clairvoyance is *clairaudience*, which is the ability to receive extrasensory information as sound. *Clairsentience* is another form of clairvoyance in which the recipient experiences extrasensory information in a more generalized feeling sense. Investigatively, clairvoyance is used primarily to help locate suspects and missing persons or objects, such as murder weapons.

Remote viewing is the ability to describe remote objects, events, or places using something other than the known five senses. The term *remote viewing* (RV) was chosen to describe a particular kind of experimental protocol or method of which there are several different types, including Controlled Remote Viewing, Technical Remote Viewing, Scientific Remote Viewing, Extended Remote Viewing, and Associative Remote Viewing. Investigatively, remote viewers work from objects, maps, and geographical coordinates to ascertain and describe specific locations and the "profile" of an individual, subject, or situation.

Precognition is the ability to predict or intuitively know or foresee future events that cannot be inferred from present knowledge. A precognition is similar to a *premonition*, which is a forewarning of a future event. Investigatively, this ability is used proactively, e.g., to predict criminal behavior and where a missing person might be found.

Dowsing is a form of ESP in which underground water, minerals, objects (e.g. bodies, artifacts, lost articles) are located by sensitive individuals, usually with the aid of a dowsing rod or pendulum. A specific form of dowsing involves the use of maps and aerial photos in place of working on-site. This form is most often used when searching for missing persons.

Psychometry is extrasensory perception of the history of an object, including facts of the people and events connected with it, usually through physical contact with the object. Psychometry often seems to be a form of *retrocognition*, which is the ability to experience past events not in the memory of the individual undergoing the experience. The object held becomes the key to the past event or experience. Investigatively, this ability may be used to help reconstruct a crime by a psychic handling items of physical evidence or visiting the crime scene itself. Often information can be obtained regarding the perpetrator's *modus operandi*, motive, and description.

All of the above abilities have been tested scientifically, and some of the results have been astounding. When laboratory evidence is lacking (which is sometimes the case because some psychic abilities and phenomena cannot be generated on demand), there is a wealth of anecdotal and well-documented experiences by credible persons. The authors' purpose here is not to exhaustively review the evidence for psychic abilities but merely to give the reader a glimpse of some of the more conclusive scientific research and persuasive anecdotal material. In a nutshell, the case for psi is summarized by Dr. Dean Radin, a highly regarded parapsychologist: "Psi has been shown to exist in thousands of experiments. There are disagreements over how to interpret the evidence, but the fact is that virtually all scientists who have studied the evidence, *including the hard-nosed skeptics*, now agree that something interesting is going on that merits serious scientific attention." Similarly, after studying the evidence for three decades, Dr. Broughton is convinced that "there is an enormous amount of evidence for what we call psychic ability that remains to be explained and understood. . . . Hundreds and hundreds of experiments in parapsychology have provided good evidence of psi phenomena."

TELEPATHY

"I must suggest to you that you should think more kindly of the objective possibility of thought-transference and therefore also of telepathy," wrote Sigmund Freud, the founder of psychoanalysis and a staunch skeptic of supernatural beliefs. Interestingly, this statement was made before any of the many scientific experiments were done that confirmed the existence of telepathy.

Telepathy was first seriously studied scientifically in Dr. Rhine's laboratory. A "sender" would randomly select a single card from a deck of ESP cards (a standard pack of twenty-five cards with five cards each of five symbols: star, circle, square, cross, and three parallel wavy lines) and attempt to "send" the image to a "receiver." Dr. Rhine found that some subjects' scores were so high that the odds of scoring that well by chance were a million to one. One particularly gifted nineteen-year-old girl guessed twenty-three of twenty-five cards correctly in an experiment at her school and later guessed all twenty-five correctly when tested under laboratory conditions at Duke University.

According to Dr. Radin, from 1974 to 1997 some 2,549 *Ganzfeld* sessions (a particular form of telepathy experiment), reported in some forty publications by researchers from laboratories around the world, established that "we are fully justified in having very high confidence that people sometimes get small amounts of specific information from a distance without the use of the ordinary senses."

Researchers at the Stanford Research Institute in Menlo Park, California, demonstrated that the brain waves of two subjects isolated by a Faraday cage (an enclosure that shields a person from normal electromagnetic signals) could be synchronized. A light pulsed in the eyes of one subject would cause a distinct electroencephalogram (EEG) pattern. The second subject, when instructed to think about the first subject, would suddenly acquire the same distinct EEG pattern.

Two ophthalmologists at Jefferson Medical College in Philadelphia demonstrated that a change in brain rhythm, such as the production of alpha waves, in one identical twin could cause a matching shift in the brain of the other twin. Similarly, an electrochemist at the Newark College of Engineering demonstrated that when someone concentrates on a person's name with whom he has an emotional tie, the distant subject registers a measurable change in blood pressure and volume. Research showed that one of every four people has this sensitivity. He also demonstrated with a simple form of emotional Morse code that messages could be transmitted telepathically as far as 1,200 miles. Similarly, Russian scientists have successfully used brain waves as carriers of information by transmitting a name from a sender in Moscow to a receiver in Leningrad. A similar experiment was conducted by Thelma Moss, a medical psychologist and assistant professor at the Neuropsychiatric Institute, UCLA. She attempted transmitting a series of images and sounds displayed to senders in Los Angeles to receivers in New York and England. In one of the more striking examples, a series of slides and sounds of satellites and rocket ships in flight was shown to the sender. One receiver in England wrote back: "I could see the world as if I were in a space ship." Another English receiver wrote: "*War of the Worlds,* H.G. Wells? Or the next war involving death by the use of satellites and flying platforms."

A considerable amount of research has been conducted on telepathy and dreams. Dr. Stanley Krippner, while director of the Maimonides Hospital Division of Parapsychology and Psychophysics, discovered that telepathic senders concentrating on target material such as pictures, sounds, and objects were able to directly influence the dreams of sleeping research subjects.

Besides the overwhelming scientific evidence, there are literally thousands of anecdotal records of telepathic communication between two emotionally bonded people. For example, in 1879 Sir John Drummond Hay, Queen Victoria's minister to Morocco, was awakened by his daughter-in-law's anguished voice, although she was 300 miles away. The voice cried, "Oh, I wish papa only knew that Robert is ill." A few minutes later he heard the plea again. He recorded the experience in his diary but was not concerned because he did not believe in telepathy, and he knew that his son, Robert, was in good health at their last meeting. Later, Sir John found out that his son had been stricken by typhoid fever, and his son's wife had repeated the exact phrase that woke him that very same night.

Many cases involve telepathic communication between close friends when one is involved in a disaster. For instance, a Soviet sailor reported the following occurrence:

> While serving on a submarine I became ill, and the ship had to leave without me. During an afternoon nap I had the following dream: I was right back on the submarine, standing on the deck. The boat began to descend

into the water, but I was unable to reach the conning tower and make my way down into the safety of the ship; I was overwhelmed by the water, began to swallow it, and felt that I was drowning. At this point I awoke sweating and with my pulse racing. I remembered the dream quite vividly afterward. When the submarine returned to its base and I rejoined the crew, I heard that one of my comrades had drowned. He had accidentally remained on deck while the boat submerged. When I checked the ship's log, I discovered that the accident had happened at the very moment I experienced the nightmare of my own drowning.

CLAIRVOYANCE

After a comprehensive review of the experimental evidence for clairvoyance, Dr. Radin concluded that "the evidence demonstrates that psi perception operates between minds and through space," in some instances demonstrating odds against chance of ten million to one.

At the Stanford Research Institute Uri Geller, the famous Israeli psychic, was asked by two physicists to reproduce a total of thirteen drawings while physically shielded from the experimenters in a double-walled steel room that was secure acoustically, visually, and electrically. After isolating Geller, the experimenters retired to another room where they randomly selected a target picture and drew it. Examples of selected drawings included a cluster of grapes, a house, a bridge, and a kite. Two independent researchers were asked to judge the results by matching the drawings done by the experimenters with Geller's reproductions. The judges easily matched all the drawings with no errors, which had a statistical chance probability of one in a million per judgment.

In another experiment, Geller was asked to guess the face of a die shaken vigorously in a closed steel box. Of ten guesses Geller provided the correct answer eight times and refused to respond two times, saying that his perception was not clear. This was a triple-blind experiment, because no one knew the actual fall of the die until the box was opened, hence ruling out telepathy.

Another study involving the clairvoyant perception of ordinary playing cards yielded results that ruled out chance. A test subject was asked to make "confidence calls" (predictions by the subject of the most accurate guesses) when trying to identify randomly selected cards. Of the subject's twenty-five confidence calls, all twenty-five were correct.

Norman Shealy, a neurosurgeon and former director of the Rehabilitation Center in LaCrosse, Wisconsin, found in a carefully controlled experiment that three clairvoyants tested were 80 percent correct in diagnosing physical illness when only provided with the names, birth dates, and pictures of the patients.

As part of a study conducted by Charles Tart, professor emeritus of psychology at the University of California at Davis, a young woman was hooked up to sophisticated physiological equipment and slept in a psychophysiological laboratory. A five-digit random number was placed on a shelf high above her head, and she was visually monitored through an observation window. Her task was to read the number psychically, memorize it, and report it upon waking. She could not do this by ordinary means, because any physical movement would be immediately seen or detected by the equipment. Upon waking she correctly reported the number (25132). The odds against guessing the number were 100,000 to 1. The actual psychic ability used to perceive the number in this instance is open to question, however. The subject could have seen it clairvoyantly, received the number telepathically from the experimenter (because he knew what it was), or had an out-of-the-body experience, as she claimed. Whichever is true, the result is equally impressive.

In a scientific test of the psychic abilities of three aborigines from northern New South Wales, a psychologist in conjunction with Sydney University asked each to describe the contents of a sealed box ten miles away (the box contained a cigarette). One aborigine said the box contained a cigarette, and the other two said tobacco and paper. In another test a cigarette holder was added to the box (an item none of the test subjects had ever seen before), and nine out of the ten aborigines tested accurately described the shape, length, and color of the object.

As with telepathy, there is a wealth of personal anecdotal experiences that amply demonstrate the existence of clairvoyance. The following account is by a South African hunter and merchant who described his experience in 1875 in his privately printed book, *Among the Zulu and the Amatongos:*

I had sent out my native elephant hunters with instructions to meet me at a certain date at a selected spot. I arrived there at the appointed time, but none of my hunters had put in an appearance. Having nothing much to do, I went to see a native doctor who had a great reputation, just to amuse myself and see what the man would say. At first the doctor refused to tell anything, because, as he said, he had no knowledge of white men's affairs. At last he consented and said he would "open the gates of distance and travel through it," even though it should cost him his life.

He then demanded the names and number of the hunters. I demurred at first, but finally did as requested. The doctor then made eight fires, one for each hunter, and cast into them roots which burned with a sickly smelling smoke. The man took some medicine and fell into a trance for about ten minutes, his limbs moving all the time.

When he came around from the trance, he raked out the ashes of his first fire and described the appearance of the man represented by it and said, "This man has died of fever, and his gun is lost." He then said that the second hunter had killed four elephants and described the shape and size of the tusks. He said that the next had been killed by an elephant, but the gun was coming home alright. Then he described the appearance and fortunes of the next, adding that the survivors would not be home for three months and would travel by a road different from that agreed upon. The prediction turned out correct in every particular, and, as the hunters were scattered over country over 200 miles away, the man could hardly have obtained news of them from other natives, nor did the diviner know that he was going to be consulted.

REMOTE VIEWING

Remote viewing is the capacity of some people, known as *viewers*, to accurately describe unknown objects, events, and geographical locations. In other words, a viewer needs no physical or tangible connection to gain information about a distant subject or *target*. RV works whether the target is in the next room or the other side of the planet. Research shows that time, space, or any other kind of "shielding" (such as an electronically shielded room) cannot prevent a good remote viewer from gaining access to a desired target. Remote viewers tend to differentiate themselves from clairvoyants or psychics. According to Paul Smith "a trained, experienced remote viewer will provide demonstrated contact with a target consistently more often than the average 'natural' psychic." This notwithstanding, the original RV researchers are clear in their belief that remote viewing is a psychic ability. And parapsychologist Dean Radin considers it a form of clairvoyance.

In their book, *The Mind Race*, veteran RV researchers Russell Targ and Keith Harary explain that

> remote viewing is primarily an ability to process pictorial, nonanalytic information. For example, if an experienced viewer were working with the police, looking for a kidnap victim, he might be able to describe the location or house where the kidnap victim was being held, but would be much less likely to provide a correct street address. Names, numbers, letters, and other analytic material are among the most difficult information for viewers to describe.

How well does RV work? According to Smith, there are "two extreme claims about remote viewing. One says it does not work. The other says it works all the time. The truth is really in between, although closer to the positive end of the scale. After long practice, experienced viewers can access a target nearly one hundred percent of the time. This does not mean their data is 100 percent accurate, nor does it mean they get all the data they were looking for. All it means is that they retrieve information indicating that they were 'there.' However, these experienced viewers regularly obtain extremely accurate, often error-free information from the target." Close scientific scrutiny of RV in scores of studies has revealed a 66 percent reliability, which is statistically highly significant, beating the odds of chance by 100 to 1.

Historically, RV dates from a number of pioneering experiments performed under the auspices of the American Society for Psychical Research (ASPR) by New York artist and psychical researcher Ingo Swann in the early 1970s. With remarkable successes at the ASPR, Swann teamed up with Dr. Hal Puthoff at Stanford Research Institute's (SRI) Radio Physics Laboratory in Menlo Park, California. Working together, Puthoff, Swann and others conducted a series of even more sophisticated experiments developing the approach they ultimately dubbed *remote viewing* in 1972 (although in hindsight some believe that *remote sensing* might have been a more correct term).

According to Dr. Puthoff and collaborator Russell Targ, an experimental physicist, the scientific research endeavor at SRI might never have been supported had it not been for three apparent operational successes in the early days of the program. One success concerned the

"West Virginia Site," in which two remote viewers purportedly identified a secret underground facility. One of them apparently named code words and personnel in this facility accurately enough that it launched a security investigation to determine how the information could have been leaked. Based only on the coordinates of the site, the viewers described the above-ground terrain, then proceeded to describe details of the hidden underground site.

One of the same viewers then claimed that he could describe a similar Communist Bloc site and proceeded to do so for a site in the Ural Mountains. According to Puthoff and Targ, "the two reports for the West Virginia Site, and the report for the Urals Site were verified by personnel in the sponsor organization as being substantially correct."

The third reported operational success concerned an accurate description of a large crane and other information at a site in Semipalatinsk, in the former USSR. Again, the viewer was provided only with the geographical coordinates of the site and was asked to describe what was there.

Although some of the information in these examples was verified as highly accurate, the evaluation of operational work remains difficult, in part because there is no chance baseline for comparison (as there is in controlled experiments) and in part because of differing expectations of different evaluators. For example, a government official who reviewed the Semipalatinsk work concluded that there was no way the remote viewer could have drawn the large gantry crane unless "he actually saw it through remote viewing, or he was informed of what to draw by someone knowledgeable of [the site]." Yet that same analyst concluded that "the remote viewing of [the site] by subject S1 proved to be unsuccessful [because] the only positive evidence of the rail-mounted gantry crane was far outweighed by the large amount of negative evidence noted in the body of this analysis." In other words, the analyst had the expectation that to be "successful" a remote viewing should contain *only* accurate information, a decidedly unrealistic expectation.

These experiments by Swann at SRI soon attracted the attention of the Central Intelligence Agency (the CIA had been studying psi since 1952 and its potential applications in the Cold War). Revelations from behind the Iron Curtain indicated that the Soviets were not only heavily financing experiments in various psychic phenomena, but that they were having considerable success with their research program. The

CIA wanted to know what the Soviets were researching and finding that could be a threat to the national security of the United States. The CIA also believed that RV might be useful to the U.S. defense program. Eventually, representatives from the CIA brought a few select projects to SRI for which it wanted answers, and tasked Swann and another remote viewer, Pat Price (a former police commissioner and vice-mayor of Burbank, California), with the project. The results in some cases were spectacular and in all cases sufficiently intriguing that the CIA came back repeatedly for more. For instance, the CIA wanted to find out if a psychic could see a remote location and accurately describe specific military installations there. Using Swann and Price, SRI provided the CIA with descriptions of military bases in Russia and China that were later confirmed by intelligence ground checks. As another part of this project, dubbed Project Scanate, Pat Price provided a detailed description of a top-secret American satellite tracking station, including names of officers and operations code words. The only information given Price were the geographical coordinates. Unfortunately, in the mid-1970s a number of scandals involving the CIA forced it to divest itself of any sort of controversial activities in which it was engaged at that time.

Consequently, the program was passed on to the Defense Intelligence Agency (DIA) under a program called Grill Flame. A few smaller programs administered by military services and other agencies were contained under the Grill Flame umbrella. Among them was the Army's program, which began in 1978 as a counterintelligence effort, with the mission of evaluating how vulnerable the United States was to psychic spying. So successful was the effort that the Department of Defense (DOD) and Army officials decided to change the emphasis from assessing vulnerabilities to actively collecting intelligence against America's cold war adversaries. The idea of psychic spies, however, was not especially popular among many generals, upper-level bureaucrats, and politicians. By the early 1980s, the DIA had scaled back, but not totally dropped, its Grill Flame effort.

In 1980, the Army itself lost all funding for the RV program. However, Major General Bert Stubblebine, commander of the Army's Intelligence and Security Command (INSCOM)—parent headquarters for the organization controlling the RV unit—took a personal and active interest in the psi program. In 1983 he directed that the program be redesignated the INSCOM Center Lane Program, and be funded directly from INSCOM's budget, i.e., "out-of-hide," in military parlance.

Swann and the SRI team had developed an improved version of remote viewing known as *coordinate remote viewing* (CRV). Around the time of the debut of Center Lane, the Army and SRI signed contracts to train five military and DOD civilian personnel in the new remote viewing technique at SRI facilities. In 1986, INSCOM transferred the unit to DIA and changed its name to Sun Streak. Early in the 1990s it went through yet another name change, to Stargate, the name by which it became known to the world when the program was declassified in December 1995. During the program's lifetime, the remote viewing unit collected intelligence about a broad range of foreign targets, including strategic missile forces, political leaders, narcotics operations, research and development facilities, hostage situations, military weapons systems, secret installations, technology developments, terrorist groups–the list was staggering and the successes were many.

However, Congress directed the CIA to take back the responsibility for the program from the DIA in 1995, but the CIA did not want it. Under the guise of an "objective" study by the American Institutes for Research, a Washington think tank, the CIA commissioned the services of one of the most anti-psi skeptics in the country and contrived to skew the assessment such that the RV program would seem to have been useless as an intelligence-gathering effort. In its final Stargate incarnation, the CIA canceled the RV program in mid 1995.

Actual declassified remote viewing case files will be presented in Chapter 6, PSI CASEFILES.

PRECOGNITION

Precognition has been demonstrated and replicated successfully in many different laboratories and experiments. Parapsychologist Charles Honorton and psychologist Diane Ferrari analyzed 309 precognition experiments conducted by sixty-two different researchers and reported in 113 articles published from 1935 to 1987. The combined results produced odds against chance of ten million billion billion to one! In other words, the element of chance was totally eliminated as an explanation for successful precognitions.

Many of the standard telepathy experiments involving the attempt of a subject to identify a card known only to the experimenter have been altered to test precognition, with results often nearly as good as those for telepathy. In these experiments the subject is asked to guess the cards *before* they are chosen. In a more sophisticated version of this experimental protocol, subjects are asked to predict target information before it is selected by a computer. Some subjects have succeeded to a highly statistically significant degree.

Most evidence for precognition, however, comes from anecdotal records. Bulgarian psychic Vanga Dimitrova (mentioned in Chapter 2) was determined to have an 80 percent accuracy rate in predicting highly specific and unique future events. She is particularly accurate in predicting the exact date of peoples' deaths. Edgar Cayce, America's most famous seer, did literally thousands of psychic readings on peoples' futures, most of which were reportedly very accurate. Mrs. Eileen Garrett became famous overnight for her precognition of the R-101 airship disaster and others in the 1930s. Arthur Ford, a medium, became famous for obtaining lists of soldiers killed in action during World War II before their deaths actually occurred. Mrs. Jeane Dixon correctly forecasted in print all the presidential elections from 1928 to 1968. She also correctly predicted the exact date–February 20, 1947– as the date of the partition of Pakistan and India several months before it happened.

An interesting case of an apparently unwitting precognition involved the publication of *The Titan*, by Morgan Robertson in 1898, fourteen years before the fateful maiden voyage of the Titanic. The novel describes in uncanny detail what was to be the fate of the Titanic, yet this was long before the Titanic was even conceived of. The plot of the novel deals with the sinking of the Titan on its maiden voyage, and many of its details are almost identical with the actual statistics of the Titanic, e.g., the length and weight of the ship, number of its propellers, engine power, top speed, the number of passengers and lifeboats, time of sailing, and the place and nature of the disaster. Interestingly, Robertson said that the ideas for his stories came to him as visions while in a trance. He believed that the visions were given to him by an "astral writing partner."

Another illustrative precognitive case reported in the literature involved the district manager of a sheet and tin plate company. While on a fishing trip in the deep woods of Canada with no means of communication, he dreamt of an accident at his plant involving a crane that had toppled over from lifting too heavy a load of scrap metal, damaging several railroad cars. In his dream he saw the damage done, including the numbers on the crane and railroad cars. On returning to his plant, he discovered that the damage corresponded perfectly with his dream, even to the numbers dreamt. The dream occurred approximately two hours before the accident.

Precognitive dreams are not as unusual as one might think, although the concept is contrary to our entrenched belief in linear time. For instance, there are many authenticated accounts of people repeatedly dreaming the winners of horse races, often by nonbettors and nonracing enthusiasts. In one case, an educational psychologist dreamt the winners of races three or four times a week for almost four months. In the dreams the woman would hear the race announcer give the winning horse's name, even though she was not interested in horse racing and never even heard of the horse's name before.

Some of the best evidence for precognitive dreams is the well-documented anecdotal accounts of famous historical personalities. Foremost among these is probably President Lincoln's well-known dream of his own assassination a few weeks before it happened. Calpurnia dreamt that Caesar fell bleeding across her knees and warned him not to go out on the day he was stabbed twenty-three times. More frequently, precognitive dreams concern disasters befalling other people. A typical example is recorded in Mark Twain's biography: "One night when Mark Twain was at his sister's house in St. Louis, he dreamed that Henry, his brother, was a corpse lying in a metallic burial case in their sister's sitting room, supported on two chairs with a bouquet of flowers and a single crimson bloom in the center of his chest. Next morning he told his sister the dream. A few weeks later Henry's ship's boilers blew up and he later died exactly as in the dream."

Other tragic events such as the assassinations of John and Robert Kennedy and Martin Luther King, Chappaquiddick, Egyptian President Nasser's fatal heart attack, the fatal airplane crash of Rocky Marciano, the sinking of the Titanic and an Onassis tanker, and the deaths of Krushchev and Stravinsky were all accurately predicted and recorded before the fact in the files of the Central Premonitions Registries in New York and London. Other well-documented accounts include the warning of King Alexander of Serbia and his wife, Queen Draga, of their assassination through a séance. And the assassination of Count Tisza, the Prime Minister of Hungary, was forseen by his wife.

DOWSING

Although as little understood as any of the other psychic abilities, the practical application of dowsing has been most clearly realized and hence used. Many major water and pipeline companies have admitted employing dowsers for years. A dowser is on the payroll of the Canadian Ministry of Agriculture, UNESCO uses the services of a dowser-geologist, and engineers for the First and Third Marine Divisions in Vietnam were trained to dowse for booby traps, mines, bunkers, hidden arms caches, military targets, and enemy tunnels. In Czechoslovakia the army has a special permanent corp of dowsers. In Russia, where research on dowsing is state financed, the geology departments of Moscow State and Leningrad University are conducting full-scale investigations into dowsing. Their concern is not whether or not it works, because they are convinced that it does, but how it works.

Perhaps America's best known dowser is Henry Gross, who on many occasions has located oil, water, and minerals by dowsing maps when conventional geological techniques failed. In Kansas he located thirty-six oil wells and fifteen of the seventeen drilled produced oil. Interestingly, seismic predictions of the seventeen sites were wrong in nine cases. Gross is even credited with locating missing people by using only a map.

There have been many cases reported in which dowsers have located missing persons, criminals, and bodies by dowsing a map. For example, a dowser accurately located the hideout on a city map of the two men responsible for stealing two million francs from the safe of the Societé Technique des Sables de la Seine in Paris. Another dowser pinpointed on a road map the location of the shelter of two University of Maine students caught in a severe late-season blizzard in New Hampshire's White Mountains. And a captain in the Vietnamese Navy in 1974 located on a large map a junk believed by Interpol to be carrying six tons of opium. The captain, using a pendulum, correctly predicted that only two tons of opium would be found and specified the date and time it would be seized.

In England, dowsers accurately determine the sex of humans from only a drop of blood or saliva on a piece of blotting paper, and they have been used by police forensic laboratories to assist in murder investigations.

Studies of dowsers have uncovered some interesting experimental evidence that shows that they are unusually sensitive to minute electromagnetic changes and can even detect an artificial field only 0.02 the strength of the earth's field. The Laboratoire de Physique in Paris demonstrated that dowsers could tell if an electric current was switched on or off in a coil at a distance of three feet.

PSYCHOMETRY

Ironically, this psychic ability is probably the easiest to test, yet it has been given little attention by parapsychologists. In fact, it has received more attention and testing from archaeologists than parapsychologists, because the ability has tremendous potential as an archaeological research tool. One particular area of application involves "cultural reconstruction." In this application a psychic is first tested by having him or her psychometrize an archaeological artifact about which much is known by the archaeologist, but not the psychic. If the psychic can accurately describe the history of the artifact relative to what is actually known about it, the psychic is then asked to psychometrize artifacts about which little if anything is known. In this fashion psychic archaeologists attempt to reconstruct ancient cultures and civilizations. Similarly, in criminology, the investigator can use a psychometrist to reconstruct a crime event, especially if there is a lack of witnesses and evidence.

As an example of what can occur when a good psychic psychometrizes an artifact, George McMullen, a well-known Canadian psychic, was handed a small piece of argillite at a Canadian Archaeological Association banquet in 1973. The stone was excavated at a site on the Queen Charlotte Islands and was believed to have been worked by the local Indians. McMullen, however, insisted that the stone had been carved by a black man from Port-au-Prince in the Caribbean, who had been brought to Canada as a slave, all of which was deemed to be absurd by those present at the banquet. In a subsequent reading, McMullen added that the black man was born and raised in West Africa, captured by slavers and taken to the Caribbean Islands, sold to the English, shipped to British Columbia, then escaped the ship and found refuge in a friendly Indian tribe, where he married and lived the rest of his life. It was here that he carved the argillite. Subsequent research confirmed the story.

In 1980, the authors brought McMullen to Montana to work on several, unsolved homicides. During his stay, a fisherman found a human mandible nearby in the Missouri River. The coroner, a sergeant in the sheriff's office, showed it to McMullen. Handling it only briefly, McMullen became very pensive and began to pace back and forth. Then he spoke: "Indian, male, killed by a blow to the back of the head and thrown in the river, 1803 or 4." Examination by a physical anthropologist later confirmed that the mandible did in fact belong to a Native American man and that it had been buried for well over a 100 years.

• • •

In sum, Dr. Radin concludes that the evidence for telepathy, clairvoyance, precognition and other psi phenomena "is so well-established that most psi researchers today no longer conduct 'proof-oriented' experiments." He goes on to say that "we've learned that the effects observed in a thousand psi experiments [have] been independently replicated by competent, conventionally trained scientists at well-known academic, industrial, and government-supported laboratories worldwide for more than a century, and the effects are consistent with human experiences reported throughout history and across all cultures."

Similarly, Professor Jessica Utts of the University of California at Davis, Division of Statistics, recently conducted a scientific examination of two decades of research on psychic functioning "to determine whether or not the phenomenon has been scientifically established. . . . Using the standards applied to any other area of science, it is concluded that psychic functioning has been well established." After her extensive statistical and methodological review of numerous studies, Professor Utts concluded: "It is clear . . . that anomalous cognition is possible and has been demonstrated. This conclusion is not based on belief, but rather on commonly accepted scientific criteria. The phenomenon has been replicated in a number of forms across laboratories and cultures." In light of the evidence, Professor Utts believes that "it would be wasteful of valuable resources to continue to look for proof." She argues that "There is little benefit to continuing experiments designed to offer proof, since there is little more to be offered to anyone who does not accept the current collection of data." Furthermore, several government reports have all reached favorable conclusions regarding the existence of psi phenomena, including a 1982 Congressional Research Service report, a 1985 report prepared for the Army Research Institute, a 1987 National Research Council report requested by the United States Army, a 1989 Office of Technology Assessment report, and a 1995 report by the American Institutes for Research.

Even though psychic abilities have been repeatedly demonstrated and validated both scientifically and anecdotally, modern science lacks an adequate theory to explain how and why it works. Many books have been written by many different types of scientists, each of which presents a different theory. Ironically, it is the hardest of the hard sciences—physics—that may provide a concrete answer. Present-day physicists have discovered new and smaller subatomic particles that do not behave as particles are supposed to. The Newtonian theory of solid particles governed by immutable physical laws has been superseded by quantum theory, which basically states that the objective, deterministic, mechanical world in time and space does not exist on the subatomic level. According to Dr. Broughton, "a small but influential number of physicists think that psi phenomena already have a place in quantum physics." (Some physicists, in fact, are suggesting a new term, *paraphysics*, which is the study of the physics of paranormal processes.) Dr. Radin believes that through quantum physics "our understanding of the physical world is becoming more compatible with psi." New theories based on quantum physics speak of parallel universes interpenetrating ours, matter as energy directed by consciousness, physical objects as connected nonlocally in ways that transcend the limitations of space and time, curvatures and warps in space-time, instantaneous effects caused by events at great distances, the direct transmission of energy from brain to brain regardless of distance, morphogenetic fields that invisibly link all members of a species, and hypothetical particles called *psitrons* that convey information paranormally. The famous theologian-scientist and author, Teilhard de Chardin, stated that "modern physics is no longer sure whether what is left in its hands is pure energy or, on the contrary, pure thought." The father of modern parapsychology, J. B. Rhine, asked: "Why, indeed, should we suppose there could be no kinds of energy beyond those that are now known? Why should it be assumed that all the energies of nature be subject to time and space or be interceptible by the sensory organs of man?" And the father of modern psychology, William James, stated that "the world of our present consciousness is only one out of many worlds of consciousness that exist."

In short, it seems likely that physics may be able to provide an acceptable theory of psi in the future. Until that time we must remain content in the understanding that, with the progression of science, we can expect "the gradual normalization of what we now call paranormal . . . , understanding that which was not understood before," to quote Dr. Broughton. Psychologist T. X. Barber speculates that some "phenomena now included under parapsychology will be viewed as part of normal psychology in the near or distant future," much as mesmerism and hypnotism were once considered subfields of psychical research but are now understood to involve normal psychological processes. Dr. Barber further suggests that humans may possess certain senses that "have not as yet been categorized and understood, somewhat in the same way as the echolocation sense in bats, the magnetic sense in bees, and the electric sense in mormyrid fish were not understood until relatively recently." Astronaut Edgar Mitchell reached a similar conclusion after his extensive investigation of parapsychology in his book, *Psychic Exploration: A Challenge for Science*: "The consciousness of man has an 'extended' nature, which enables him to surpass the ordinary bounds of space and time."

There is one particularly apt analogy that may help the investigator to accept and understand the existence of psi. Physicists know that the universe is composed of energy in different states of vibration. Even dense physical objects such as rocks and steel, which we normally consider totally inanimate, are energy vibrating at a very low rate. Conceive of the universe as an infinite keyboard of vibration, and through our physical senses we are aware of only one octave somewhere in the middle. In physical terms, physicists know that the entire electromagnetic spectrum ranges in wavelength from a billionth of a centimeter to millions of miles, yet only 380 to 760 billionths of a meter is visible to us. So what we actually perceive is clearly not all of reality; it is only a very tiny slice. Psi phenomena and abilities, then, can be thought of as those lying outside our "normal range" of perception and experience, which is just one octave of a vastly broader scale. It may be, as some parapsychologists have suggested, that the senses actually serve to restrict or keep out all but the narrow band of frequencies that we perceive, because this is all that is needed to navigate and survive in our world. Furthermore, they suggest that if the senses did not restrict the influx of stimuli, we would be hopelessly overwhelmed, even driven insane, by the confusion. The implication, then, is that psychics, for whatever reason, are sensitive to a greater range of frequencies than the average person.

Someone said that there is no such thing as the supernatural, only an infinite number of possible natures. What we normally consider supernatural is not that at all; rather, it is simply that which is not yet understood and explainable. As with magic tricks, once you know how it works, it is no longer magic or a trick. The supernatural or paranormal is not mysterious in itself, it is only mysterious to us, and we are the ones who *treat* it mysteriously. That which we consider supernatural or paranormal may merely be the manifestation in this world or reality of the laws of another world or reality, laws that have not yet been discovered by science. "Supernatural" and "paranormal" are merely words for that which we do not yet understand. Consider for a moment that even Einstein's theories would have been branded superstitious nonsense only a century ago. Likewise, what is considered by many to be superstitious nonsense today will be incorporated into the scientific doctrine a century from now. As Margaret Mead, the famous anthropologist and psychic archaeology sympathizer, once commented, "The whole history of scientific advancement is full of scientists investigating phenomena the Establishment did not believe were there." And as Dr. Barber summarizes the situation, the accumulating data of diverse sciences "increasingly indicate the resounding conclusion that reality, or everything we can possibly know and possibly experience, is much broader, deeper and richer than is dreamed of in our philosophy."

The concern of the investigator using psychics should not be to explain paranormal abilities; rather, from a pragmatic point of view, the important thing is that they do in fact work. The purpose of an investigator using psychics as an investigative adjunct is not to address the question of the existence of psychic abilities, but to proceed on the assumption that they do exist, for whatever reason. The fact that the electrical engineer does not know exactly what electricity is does not prevent him or her from using it. Similarly, even though no one knows exactly what gravity is does not stop the astronomer or the aerospace engineer from practical applications of its effects. Likewise, physicians who use acupuncture cannot adequately explain why it works, yet they use it because it seems to be effective. Even though there is not an adequate theory of hypnosis and no one really knows exactly how it works, that does not prevent its practical use. And even though hypnotism was once considered an unscientific and suspect practice, it is now being used as an effective investigative technique and is gaining widespread popular and professional acceptance. In a similar vein, the use of psychics in investigations may also gain respectability. Dr. Barber recommends that if we accept "the idea that virtually all of our present-day assumptions and theories will be discarded later as they are shown to be mistaken, misleading, or severely limited, we become more open to new (*really* new) data, assumptions and conceptualizations. We become more open, for instance, to anomalous data that seem to contradict 'official' viewpoints, such as the data presented by parapsychologists."

Considering the evidence for psychic phenomena cited previously, it is obviously far more unreasonable to deny its existence than what many consider the "unreasonable" belief in psychic phenomena. In other words, in the face of such evidence, it is unreasonable to maintain that psychic phenomena and abilities do not exist. Those who hold this belief simply have not looked at the evidence or are too convinced of their own limited conception of reality to accept the obvious. Most objections to psychic phenomena are based on ignorance; scientists and laymen alike rarely bother to inform themselves about things they do not want to believe and that run counter to their preconceptions. When pressured to account for psychic phenomena, critics will make many objections based on their bias that these phenomena cannot exist. Critics will attempt to discredit the investigator, ignore reports by credible laboratories, declare positive experiments hoaxes, credit positive results to chance, pay undue attention to negative results, attack the experimental procedure and statistical analysis, and twist and reinterpret the experience or experimental results, so that it correlates with what is known and accepted. In a critique of the "irrational rationalists'" attack on parapsychology, the Rockwells accuse the critics of using false categorization, personal defamation, group derogation, unsubstantiated allegations, contradictions, *nonsequiturs*, rumor and innuendo, appeals to authority, censorship, and apocalyptic rhetoric in their denouncement. The Rockwells conclude that "The 'debunkers' have thus become the very thing they claim to despise: evangelical 'true believers,' standing on unexamined faith rather than objective analysis."

Some scientists outright reject all evidence for the paranormal based on the convoluted reasoning that because they know that it is impossible and does not exist, it must be concluded that all favorable evidence is due to error and/or fraud. Many otherwise competent scientists become notoriously unscientific when confronted with evidence for the paranormal and can often be heard to exclaim, "I don't care what the evidence is, it's impossible!" Unfortunately, they behave no differently from the clergymen of centuries ago who refused to look through Galileo's telescope at the craters on the moon, because they *knew* they did not exist, because the moon, as a heavenly body, was perfect and therefore had no imperfections. Surprisingly, such attitudes did not die with the Dark Ages and the Inquisition. Unfortunately, they are alive and well and have been institutionalized in the Committee for the Scientific Investigation of Claims of the Paranormal (CSICOP). Originally formed to critically and scientifically investigate claims of the paranormal, critics argue that CSICOP is in actuality a pseudo-scientific, fundamentalist, elitist, irresponsible, special interest advocacy group whose sole intent is vehemently *condemning*–not scientifically *investigating*–any and all claims of the paranormal. "Those who favor conventional explanations for the most part have chosen to make their case by attacking the research of the psi proponents rather than by putting their own hypotheses to test in independent research. . . . The only attitude we condemn is the tendency of certain fanatics and opportunists [both pro and con] to mislead the public with oversimplifications, exaggerated claims, and sensationalism in the media," note parapsychologists Edge, Morris, Palmer, and Rush in their textbook, *Foundations of Parapsychology*. Furthermore, critics of the paranormal are guilty of changing their standard of proof. The history of parapsychological research shows that parapsychologists have responsibly improved their research methods to meet the standards of proof set forth by their critics, only to have those standards changed when successfully met. The ugly truth is that the most fanatical critics simply cannot and will not accept positive parapsychological research results. That's no different from establishing law enforcement admissions standards that, if successfully met, are changed so that the applicants are rejected.

One target of CSICOP's ridicule and *a priori* condemnation, Truzzi and Lyons note, is "any police use of persons purporting to give aid through psychic powers." Truzzi and Lyons admonish those who would reject psychic criminology out of hand: "It remains wise to *doubt* the blue sense [their term for psychic abilities used to solve crimes], but it is scientific folly to *deny* it categorically."

Some parapsychologists and others who object to CSICOP's intellectual dishonesty and scientistic bigotry, derogatorily refer to it as PsiCops, thereby unmasking its true purpose of policing and enforcing its own particular worldview (which is known as *scientism*, not science). Dr. Radin observes that

> a person's level of commitment to the current scientific worldview will determine his or her beliefs about psi. Because perception is linked so closely to one's adopted view of reality, people who do not wish to "see" psi will in fact not see it. Nor will they view any evidence for psi, scientific or otherwise, as valid. This effect should be strongest in people who are committed to a particular view, motivated to maintain it, and cleaver enough to create good rationalizations for ignoring conflicting evidence.

Critics of psychic phenomena object that they are (a) too rare, subjective, and short-lived when they do occur; (b) not quantifiable and measurable by physical apparatus and cannot be seen; (c) inconsistent and often nonrepeatable; (d) unable to be made to occur on demand, and (e) cannot be readily controlled and manipulated. (Ironically, it is probably the very way in which scientists attempt to study psychic phenomena that makes it difficult to get positive results, i.e., the objective, detached, and cold environment in which uninteresting tests are forced on subjects by disbelieving experimenters.) The whole of parapsychology is dismissed outright by many as a pseudo-science, which it clearly is not. None of these objections, however, disprove the existence of psychic phenomena and, indeed, may say more about the objector than the phenomena themselves. In the face of the evidence, one must be skeptical of the skeptics. As Dr. Broughton comments, "skepticism can go too far, and many scientists choose to deal with anomalies simply by denying their existence." It remains sadly true that even though no other science has been subjected to and survived the amount of critical scrutiny that psychic research has, it will never be generally accepted among the scientific community until it can be shown how it works and ties in with generally accepted scientific knowledge. But as Edge et al. point out,

> even if one accepts that psi is not an established fact, that is not the same as saying there are not facts in parapsychology. It is a fact that a large percentage of people have had "psychic" experiences which if taken at face value imply that they are interacting with the outside world in ways that cannot be explained by orthodox scientific theory. It is a fact that a substantial number of qualified scientists have repeatedly reported anomalies in the more controlled context of scientific experiments which likewise seem to defy such explanation.

Although most people in the United States believe in psychic phenomena (because most have had an experience of this kind or know someone who has), the scientific community is more reserved. According to a survey of 1,188 professors at colleges and universities, 9 percent said that they accepted ESP as an "established fact," and 45 percent accepted it as a "likely possibility." Another survey of 1,416 readers of the *New Scientist* revealed that 25 percent regarded ESP to be an "established fact," with an additional 42 percent declaring it to be a "likely possibility." Only 19 percent stated it was a "remote possibility," 12 percent "merely an unknown," and only 3 percent believed it to be an "impossibility." Interestingly, of those who replied that ESP was an "established fact," 51 percent of them stated that their conviction was the result of a definite personal experience. Two more recent surveys of well over 1,000 respondents each revealed that 67 percent and 75 percent, respectively, believed that ESP is a "likely possibility." The survey also showed that 88 percent of the sample believed the investigation of ESP to be "a legitimate scientific undertaking." Furthermore, many believed that too much time was spent in trying to prove the existence of ESP and that parapsychologists should accept that it does work and get on with discovering how.

There is actually considerable evidence in support of psi phenomena among some quarters of the scientific community, such as: (a) the existence of reputable professional organizations composed of scientists from many fields, such as the Society for Psychical Research, the

American Society for Psychical Research (founded in 1885 with a current membership of 2,000), the International Parapsychological Association, and The Parapsychological Association (which was formed in 1957 by professional researchers of psi phenomena, has over 280 members, and was admitted as an affiliate to the prestigious American Association for the Advancement of Science in 1969), the Parapsychology Foundation (established in 1951), and the American Association for Parapsychology (founded in 1971); (b) several colleges and universities are presently offering courses in parapsychology, a few psychology textbooks now have chapters on parapsychology, some doctoral degrees are being awarded in the field, and research is being funded by individuals, institutions, and the government; (c) conservative bastions of scientific research such as the Stanford Research Institute and the Princeton Engineering Anomalies Research Laboratory at Princeton University are conducting important ongoing studies of psychic phenomena; (d) there are numerous professional parapsychologists worldwide conducting serious research that is generally published in any of several parapsychology journals, including the *Journal of Parapsychology, Journal of the Society for Psychical Research, Journal of the American Society for Psychical Research,* and the *European Journal of Parapsychology*; and (e) well-known professional scientific journals are publishing articles favorable to psi phenomena, including *Foundations of Physics, American Psychologist, Statistical Science, Behavioral and Brain Sciences, Psychological Bulletin,* and *Physical Review.*

Regardless of the final outcome of the ongoing debate, the fact remains that if psychic abilities are to be of practical value they should be used. Parapsychological researchers in the United States (who only number approximately one dozen) are still preoccupied with attempting to prove that psychic phenomena exist. By contrast, parapsychological researchers in the former Soviet Union (who number approximately 400) assume psychic phenomena to exist and are busy seeking practical applications. As a result, American experts maintain that the Russians are fifteen to twenty years ahead of us in the research and development of psychic capabilities. Research in the former Soviet Union is openly government funded, and they have actively explored military applications of psychic abilities. They even attempt to train their cosmonauts in telepathy, so that they can communicate with the ground station in case of radio failure. Other countries such as Czechoslovakia teach their citizens to use precognition to avoid potential problems and accidents, and in Iceland and Holland people are encouraged to develop and use their psychic potential from childhood. It is precisely this attitude that the authors believe should be assumed by investigators: they should accept what has been demonstrated to exist and use it to society's advantage.

It is ironic that psychic research, although it is currently treated disparagingly by most scientists, may prove to be one of the most important endeavors in the history of science. It is *probable* that it will eventually shed an entirely new light on the true nature of mind, consciousness, and reality. And it is *likely* to eventually transform the very foundations of our materialistic science. Humankind has conquered outer space, but we actually know very little about the potentials and capacities of inner space. According to Dr. Radin, at a minimum

> genuine psi suggests that what science presently knows about the nature of the universe is seriously incomplete, that the capabilities and limitations of human potential have been vastly underestimated, that beliefs about the strict separation of objective and subjective are almost certainly incorrect, and that some "miracles" previously attributed to religious or supernatural sources may instead be caused by extraordinary capabilities of human consciousness.

Chapter 4

PRACTICAL APPLICATION

"The key question for most police," according to Dr. Truzzi, "is not whether psychics are 'real,' but whether or not they can help in furthering solutions of cases. [The issue is one] of the blue sense's utility rather than its validity." The authors concur. As we argue and attempt to demonstrate throughout this book, psychics can be useful to the investigator and therefore should be used. In this chapter we discuss how to identify, recruit, test, and use psychics to maximize the chances of success.

The ideal first step for any law enforcement or criminal justice agency interested in using psychics in criminal investigation is to decide at a command level to seriously evaluate it as an investigative tool. This may not be easy, however, because many command officers simply may not be interested. They may be outright skeptical or even hostile to the idea or fear public criticism or ridicule. They may be concerned that the involvement of psychics may jeopardize the integrity of investigations or engender a carnival atmosphere. They may also resist the idea of going outside the department for help for fear of appearing incompetent. Assuming that command level sanction is obtained, the agency should establish a program for recruiting, testing, and using psychics as an investigative adjunct according to preestablished procedures for a predetermined length of time. In other words, the agency should commit itself by being willing to devote the necessary man-hours and expertise to this examination. By not doing so, the end result of an informal and loosely structured program or approach will be inconclusive and haphazard. Unfortunately, this is all too often the case.

The next step will be to assign a sympathetic and interested officer, if there is one, to design and carry out the program. The procedures and guidelines outlined in this book are intended to serve as a model. This officer should be given the go-ahead to spend what duty time he or she believes necessary to do justice to the project. *The importance of officer attitude cannot be overemphasized.* Parapsychological research has shown repeatedly that there is a direct correlation between the experimenter's attitude and the results obtained. In other words, positive results with psychics depend on a positive attitude of the investigator. This was even recognized in *Police Chief* magazine, which recommended that the officers involved should be "fairly open-minded in regard to the existence of psychic ability. It must be remembered that while most psychics expect some skepticism concerning their abilities, hostile or overt skepticism may divert their attention and ultimately decrease their effectiveness."

These first two steps represent the ideal state of affairs and approach, yet it should be realized that only a progressive department with sympathetic and interested command officers will consider this. In only one instance that is known to the authors has such a formal study been conducted, and this was at the Los Angeles Police Department. Dr. Martin Reiser (ret.), director of their Behavioral Science Services, conducted two formal pilot studies of the use of psychics in criminal investigation and published the results (see Bibliography). Although there was a considerable number of "hits" provided by the test psychics, the results were deemed inconclusive yet warranted further study.

Unfortunately, the use of psychics by investigators is usually a much more informal and less organized approach. The norm is for one or two interested officers in a department to use psychics known to them. This may be done overtly; that is, with command level permission. For example, Det. Sgt. Keaton worked with psychics under four elected sheriffs, each granting permission for him to pursue this method of investigation, even though some didn't believe in it. It may also be done covertly. For fear of ridicule, some investigators will conceal their interest and pursue it largely on their own time. The guidelines and procedures outlined in this section, however, are just as valid and important for the informal operator to follow as they are for the formal departmental study approach.

IDENTIFYING AND RECRUITING PSYCHICS

The first task of the interested investigator is to identify potential psychics who may be able and willing to offer their time and skills. The usual pattern is to seek out the services of a "hero," i.e., a well-known professional psychic, such as those mentioned in Chapter 2. The advantage to this approach is that these psychics have a track record and do not need to be tested. The disadvantage is that it may cost the department in the form of a fee for services (although many work free of charge) and/or expenses paid (although the victim's family often will pay this). Furthermore, where well-known psychics go, the media is often not far behind.

Having explored this route for several police departments, the authors (WH & RW) developed a more practical approach. Our thesis was that each community had a number of potential psychics that could be recruited as volunteers and used on an ongoing basis as a complementary investigative tool and not merely as a last resort. Det. Sgt. Keaton, Captain Wolverton, and other police officers experienced with using psychics in criminal investigations encourage their use when a case is fresh, but only if really needed, e.g., for lack of clues and suspects.

To identify potential psychics we used several techniques. First, we would ask potentially interested officers if they knew of any psychics in town. This usually turned up a few names. Second, we would locate any health food stores and metaphysical bookshops in the area, introduce ourselves to the proprietors, and tell them of our interest, stressing the experimental nature of our project and the need for confidentiality. Almost without fail, the proprietors would give us some names of likely psychics who frequent their businesses. We would then approach these people in the same manner and get additional names from them. Within a few days we usually would have identified and talked with between one and two dozen people. Of these, all but a few were interested in working on the project.

By using this technique, which sociologists call "networking," we easily identified over a hundred psychics in several dozen cities throughout the western states. In so doing we noticed several important general characteristics. First, by using the preceding networking technique, we quickly reached saturation in the community, i.e., within a few days of interviewing, we started hearing the same names again, and there were no new names. Second, it became obvious that there are underground networks of psychics, most of whom know each other. In some communities these people are already banded together in a group that meets periodically to discuss and develop their respective talents. These groups are ideal resources to tap, because they are usually enthusiastic about being given a practical and potentially helpful outlet for their skills. Third, and most important, the people we identified were largely middle-class, responsible citizens, gainfully employed, and above all concerned about maintaining their anonymity and confidentiality. The issue of confidentiality extends both ways. The investigator must assure the psychics that their identity will be concealed (to prevent public criticism and possible criminal retribution). Similarly, the investigator must insist that the psychics respect the confidentiality of the project and the officer(s). As a result, in all our experience with psychics working on criminal cases in many different states and cities, not once was there a confidentiality breech as gauged by the barometer of media discovery.

Besides stressing confidentiality, the investigator should assure the psychic informants that a suspect cannot be arrested and convicted on the basis of psychic information, hence they will never have to testify in court. Obviously, all psychically obtained information must be corroborated to the extent that the case can stand entirely on the corroborated evidence. If a question is ever raised as to what led the investigator to the evidence, the standard reply is "a reliable confidential informant."

Some interesting historical footnotes exist. Testimony from a medium was accepted in a South African court. He had to explain the basis of his spiritualist beliefs and how his psychic ability enabled him to find the body of a missing girl. In England during September, 1831, a man testified in court that he dreamt the location of a missing piece of evidence needed to convict a murder suspect. He notified the police and took them to the location—a place he had never seen before except in his dream. Recently, a district attorney in Louisiana actually requested that the psychic—whose information led to the arrest of the two murder suspects—testify in court because he "felt it was important to present the full story to the jury to give them a full appreciation of just how fortunate the authorities were to have these people on trial." According to a report in *The National Law Journal*, Los Angeles Superior Court Judge William McGinley found "the use of the psychic was merely an investigative tool" that could not be relied on for an arrest, but "may be used to follow up additional leads." In that particular appellate case, the judge ruled that there was sufficient independent evidence to justify the arrest.

An additional valuable local resource for identifying psychics is the more esoterically oriented churches in the community, such as Spiritualist churches and Unity churches. Important individuals to contact for information regarding psychics in the community are teachers of such disciplines as yoga, meditation, and astrology. Besides the networking approach to identifying psychics locally, the investigator can contact any reputable organizations, institutions, or parapsychologists in the state or region who are involved in psychic research. In so doing, the investigator may obtain the names of tested psychics in the area, besides gaining valuable technical assistance and advice from those experienced in the field. In fact, Dr. Louise Ludwig, formerly of the L.A.P.D. Behavioral Science Services and founder of the now defunct PsiCom (a professional organization whose goal was to provide technical and training services in psychic investigation), recommends that law enforcement agencies accumulate lists of "dependable" psychics. She suggests getting recommendations from other detectives and police departments, from professional parapsychological organizations like the *American Society for Psychical Research* in New York, or parapsychological laboratories like the *Institute for Parapsychology* in Durham, North Carolina. Another source is the *Psychic Sleuths Project* in Grass Lake, Michigan.

Another potential source for locating psychic investigators is the Internet. With the Internet as a major platform for communications in a global society, psychics have flourished. Almost every experienced and recognized psychic investigator has a web page which can facilitate identifying and contacting these people. The problem is the proverbial sorting of the wheat from the chaff. The *on-line* psychic business flourishes, but its integrity is highly questionable; many of these psychics are business and marketing people first, primarily after clients and their money. It is dangerous territory. So, as always, insist on and check references and recommendations. Be cautious, careful, and thorough with the information and contacts that can be had with the click of a mouse.

The investigator approaching the people identified as psychic should expect them to be cautious—even skeptical and perhaps a little paranoid–until a certain degree of confidence and understanding has been reached. It is always important for the investigator to be honest and straightforward, because psychics of any quality will be "psyching" him or her out, i.e., intuitively evaluating them, deciding whether to become involved. It is recommended that the investigator simply describe the project and then ask the person if he or she is interested in participating. It is also recommended that the investigator explain how it is that he or she came by the psychic's name to help alleviate the paranoia factor. The investigator also should, at appropriate intervals and after a degree of trust and rapport has been established, ask the person about his or her psychic ability, such as: What particular gift or talent do you have? How long have you had it? Are you trying to develop it? Would you care to relate some of your experiences?

As a typical example of what can be expected during an initial recruiting meeting, the following encounter is offered. The authors identified a registered nurse as a potential psychic. We introduced ourselves, briefly explained our purpose, and arranged to have lunch with her. After further explaining the program and sharing some of our experiences, and after an apparent degree of rapport and trust was established, we shifted the conversation to her abilities and experiences. In response she said that her mother had been psychic and that she herself had had experiences since childhood, but that they frightened her somewhat and that she didn't really have time to actively develop them while raising a family. But now that her family was grown, she was interested in participating. In discussing her experiences she related the following episodes: Once she had left her two young children in the care of a friend so that she could leave home for awhile. When returning she was driving down the street on a clear day, no more than a block from home, when suddenly it appeared to get foggy and she "saw" her son with blood all over him. He approached her in her "vision" and said, "It's alright, Mommy, I fell down on a broken glass and got seven stitches." Arriving at her house, she was met by her excited friend and her son, who indeed was covered with blood. The mother said to her friend, "Before you say anything let me guess. He fell down on a broken glass and got seven stitches." The amazed friend asked if she had talked to the doctor, and she replied that she hadn't but somehow just knew. On another occasion the nurse's brother came over to her house before going skiing. She felt that something bad was going to happen, so she recommended that he not go. He thought her request silly and asked her to go along, because it was a nice day, but she refused. Extremely nervous all day, she finally received a phone call that her brother had been air-lifted off the ski hill with a shattered leg. At the moment of the call she intuitively knew what had happened, and on hearing the news, she relaxed and felt fine. The nurse also related how she would correctly dream of certain family members having specific problems or when anything bad happened. At the end of lunch the nurse left wanting to give psychic investigation a try, so we sent her off with a packet of solved cases (for use as test material) to work on at her leisure.

In another instance, this author interviewed a potential psychic for a case. On encountering this young woman, who had been in the marketing field, I asked her to relate how she determined that she had the skill or "gift" to work as a psychic. She related her story:

> In May of 1996 I had a dream in which I was riding in the back seat of a blue/green midsize car. My "husband" (was driving the car and in front of me in the passenger seat was his girlfriend. I was seeing through the eyes of someone else because this was not my actual husband). I knew he was having an affair with this woman, and she and I were arguing as we drove down the road. The fight grew physical and she began hitting and stabbing me. I got very scared at this point realizing I was in grave danger. I looked out the car window and saw an angel motion to me to follow her. I suddenly found myself flying over the wall of an enormous castle-looking place. I felt awe-struck and humbled to be there and relieved to be out of danger. Then I woke up.

> Three days later I read in the local newspaper that a young woman was missing and her husband and his girlfriend were suspected in her disappearance. The girlfriend had rented a blue/green Altima from a local car rental a day before the disappearance, and turned it back two days later. Blood was found in the trunk and back seat that matched the victim's. Gripped with self doubt and disbelief I waited and watched as hundreds of people gathered each weekend for search parties to find the young woman. A few weeks passed and they had still not found her. I could not stand the guilt any longer. The next step would change my life forever.

Soon after that, on a weekend search day, the young psychic approached the case detectives and citizen leader who were open to her insights. The search team showed maps to her and marked the areas that fit her description of where she said the body was (a curvy road with a trickling stream nearby). Armed with this information the victim was found later that afternoon in a ravine just a few feet from a curvy road. This author subsequently worked with this psychic with considerable success.

Experience has shown that almost without exception psychics are flattered that law enforcement officers will take them and their abilities seriously enough to ask for their assistance. Experience also has shown that most are more than happy to help. It should be remembered, however, that not all psychics have the desire or emotional makeup to be a psychic sleuth.

When searching for capable psychics, the investigator should hold any stereotypes in abeyance, because they likely will be wrong. By and large, psychics are normal people, and it must be remembered that they may be anyone or anywhere. One psychic recruit works as a clerk in a district court office, and another is the wife of an undersheriff (although he does not know that she is working on criminal cases for his own department!). Contrary to our own former stereotypes we did not encounter any black capes, crystal balls, gypsies, or witches of any kind; some strange beliefs (at least to us), yes, but outright crazies, no.

There are certain types of people who should be avoided, however, including most cultists, frustrated homemakers looking for a touch of the dramatic, attention-seeking ego-inflated seers, self-appointed "superpsychics," those seeking legitimacy and publicity, any who claim extraordinary accuracy, and most who charge money. Many psychics believe that if they were to charge for their services they would lose their skill. Furthermore, a psychic for hire is under a great deal of pressure to perform, which may stimulate a tendency to confabulate, even if subconsciously. This is not to suggest, however, that some who charge are not extremely gifted and should not be used. (Annette Martin, profiled in Chapter 2 and Chapter 6, is a case in point.) It is to suggest that one should not pay for a service that may be gotten free elsewhere. In most instances, however, where a fee is charged or there are other expenses, the victim's family is happy to pay. When this is the case, it is recommended that the psychic work directly with the investigator and not the family.

Once a potential psychic has expressed interest in participating in the project, the investigator should determine whether there are any prohibiting or interfering restrictions, such as time constraints and family obligations or objections. In some instances the families of psychics will not want them to get involved. The investigator should also do a background check on all potential recruits. Det. Sgt. Keaton agrees: "Know your psychics; that is, who they are, their track record, what other agencies or people they have worked with, and check it all out." The only justifiable time to not test a psychic is if that person already has a verifiable track record. For instance, Dr. Gary Kaufman, the forensic psychologist with the Michigan State Police, says that "If they have a proven track record of having gotten results, and can provide references of other police departments they have worked with, then you at least have something to base a judgement on."

TESTING PSYCHICS

Once a few potential psychics have been identified and recruited (any more than this becomes too unmanageable and demanding of the investigator's time), the investigator needs to make arrangements for a meeting. Ideally, he or she will have tapped into a group that already meets periodically. If not, the investigator can either form a group of those interested (which is the most efficient) or meet with each individually. This will depend on several factors, such as the wishes and convenience of the individuals (e.g., some may want to work alone), as well as the investigator's.

When the authors first began identifying and recruiting psychics to aid in criminal investigation in 1975, we quickly realized that many do not like to be tested. Some feel that testing is an affront to their "gift." If the investigator does not have faith and belief in their ability, they say, then it is not for him or her to pursue testing. Others believe that such "God-given" abilities are not to be tested, but just accepted. Still others seem to be motivated by a fear of failure. Others maintain that any effort to get consensual validation through testing automatically results in erroneous information. Yet others believe that they have already been tested enough. Many psychics are pragmatic and welcome the opportunity to test their abilities. (It is these psychics, the ones with a healthy skepticism about their abilities, that the authors prefer working with. For instance, Beverly Jaegers, one of the most respected psychic investigators, said, "I'm the biggest skeptic in the field. I believe that you can do this stuff without becoming an idiot.") Some, including the remote viewers in Buchanan's Assigned Witness

Program, offer to work an already solved case for the investigator who requests their help. "In that manner," says Buchanan, "we can show the quality of our work in a way which will allow the investigator to judge for him or herself whether we can be useful."

Once a potential psychic is recruited, it is important for the investigator to broach the matter of testing. A good way to present this is to matter-of-factly explain that this is an experimental procedure that the department is evaluating for possible long-term use. Furthermore, a great many investigative man-hours, at considerable taxpayer expense, will be devoted to following up the information obtained, so the department needs some assurance that the information is valid. A dramatic case in point occurred in 1960, when the New York Police Department's Missing Persons Unit reportedly used a bulldozer to dig a ditch "four feet deep for one square mile" on information from an untested psychic in an attempt to find the body of a missing judge, which was unsuccessful. More recently, law enforcement agencies have committed considerable manpower and equipment at great expense to pursuing psychic leads, including the use of dogs, helicopters, boats and divers, backhoes, and search parties. The psychic should also realize, it can be mentioned, that the case investigators will not likely follow up the leads provided unless they have some assurance that the psychic has provided good information in the past. In this regard, the psychic is treated the same as any informant; they are gauged strictly on the quality and reliability of their information.

At this point the investigator can simply ask the psychic his or her feelings about being tested. If they agree, then proceed with the testing procedures recommended below. If the psychic is reluctant or refuses altogether, the investigator has several options: (1) decline to work with the psychic, (2) proceed anyway and take what information one gets at face value, or (3) covertly test the psychic. The last option is recommended, because too much time may be wasted following up unreliable information from an unreliable psychic (not to mention a loss of credibility for the whole project), yet to reject the person outright may be an unnecessary loss. A simple covert testing procedure is described in the next section.

There is a strong temptation to overlook the need for testing, because it is very easy for the investigator to be swayed by the psychic's own enthusiasm and belief in their own ability; belief, however, is no substitute for hard data in criminology. As a note of caution, this is exactly what happened to the authors with our first group of six psychics. We were so taken by their sincerity, belief in their own abilities, and their enthusiasm that we quite naturally, but naively, accepted what information they gave us as likely to be true. A few "hits" from the very first session only reinforced this, and we thought we were on to a sure thing. After approximately six months of intensive work with this group (i.e., weekly meetings) and mostly disappointing results (e.g., for several months they had us searching all over the Northwest and Canada looking for a young man they said left home to run drugs, but when the ice melted he floated to the surface of a pond near his home town), we finally tested their ability, only to determine that most could not reliably determine the rudimentary question of alive or dead when shown random mugshots. At this point we disbanded the group, tested each individually, and worked only with the ones who scored significantly above chance, which we should have done at the very beginning. We learned the hard way that it is necessary to determine who is the "real McCoy" from those who only *think* they are psychic or *want* to be psychic. Testing also immediately screens out any charlatans and hucksters. A maxim to follow is: *a psychic is not a psychic until proven to be one.*

Procedures

1. Formal testing is best begun by presenting the psychics with solved cases. The investigator can prepare three or four packets, including the victims' names, addresses, locations of the crime, photos of the victims, photos of the crime scenes, and items of physical evidence. Depending on how each individual works (some only want the name, others want pictures, others need some physical evidence to hold, etc.), the investigator gives what information or items are requested by each. Some will simply want to hold the packet without knowing anything. Without supplying any details other than the bare essentials, the investigator should ask the following type of questions: What type of crime is it? How did it happen? What was the motive? Who did it? The psychics' responses can then be checked and scored against what is actually known. This procedure is easily altered for a covert test simply by informing the psychic(s) that the cases are unsolved.

As an example of what can happen with this procedure, the authors were testing a group of four new female psychic recruits–all middle-aged, employed mothers. We were prepared with several envelopes, one of which contained some items of a young female murder victim, including a credit card, a bobby pin, some head hair, and a piece of blood-soaked clothing, all from her body. The woman was attacked in her home, raped, and stabbed in the chest. The psychics, who preferred not to know what was in the envelope, had no idea what kind of case it was. The first woman took the envelope, held it in her hands for a moment, and said, "I see rape," and then passed it on to the next woman who said, "I see a young woman, very panicked, backing away quickly." The third woman, after holding the envelope for a moment, said, "I see murder, a stabbing." She passed the envelope on to the last woman, who dropped it to the floor as soon as she touched it exclaiming, "That's too hot for me to handle!"

In another instance, this author gave only the names and dates of deaths of three people to a new recruit. She thought for a moment and correctly stated that one individual got angry and killed the other two, then committed suicide.

In yet another instance, this author recruited a relatively experienced psychic, who was new to psychic investigation, to work on the mysterious disappearance of a young man. On providing the psychic with merely the man's first name she went into a trance, then jolted out of it saying that she was experiencing pain in her right fingers. She asked if this missing person was in trouble with the Mafia, because she felt broken fingers were related to the Mafia's way of handling business. I suspected immediately that this psychic had some skill, because one of the primary reasons for the man's disappearance was that he was being pursued and/or threatened by someone from New Jersey with alleged ties to organized crime.

2. Another good test is for the investigator to prepare a photo line-up of known offenders and ask each psychic to tell all they can about each, such as type of offender, personality, etc. A variation of this procedure is to individually ask each psychic to pick out the person responsible for a specific major crime known to have been committed by him.

3. A similar technique is for the investigator to select some mugshots of known offenders, some of whom are alive and at large, some in prison, and others dead. The task for the psychics is to accurately determine the status of each.

4. Potential psychics can be tested by taking them to the scene of a crime, then comparing impressions gained with facts known only to the police. (However, this is inherently risky if the crime was violent [see Precautions and Considerations below]). This is precisely what Det. Sgt. Keaton did to test Annette Martin. He took her to Mt. Tamalpais, the location of the then-recent trailside serial murders. Case details had not been made public, and Martin was told only that a woman was found on Mt. Tam off a hiking trail, the victim of a homicide. She was not told how the victim was killed, the location of the body, or any other facts of the case. Walking down the trail, Keaton deliberately walked past the place where the victim's body had been found. Several hundred feet past, Martin stopped and said, "We've gone past it, haven't we? She was found back there." Keaton asked her to lead the way. Martin walked back up the trail, turned off the trail approximately 40 yards, then sat down within a few yards of where the body was actually found. Martin then correctly said that the victim had been shot in the back of the head, details that only the police knew. Based on this accurate test, Keaton proceeded to use Martin on numerous homicides and other cases over the next two decades.

In a similar instance, Chief Graff drove psychic Bill Ward down a road where a body was found five or six months prior, stopping near three large trees. Unbeknownst to Ward, the crime involved a young lady of the evening. Graff asked, "Hey Bill, do you feel anything here?" "Should I?" "Well, I'm going to let you know that there was a murder in this general area. Do you feel anything?" Ward paused a moment and said, "It has something to do with those trees, I know that." Graff didn't know if he was signalling Ward by looking that way so he says, "Yah, that tree right there," pointing to a particular tree. Ward looked at Graff sternly and says, "Don't mess with me." "What are you talking about?" Graff asks. Ward reiterated, "Don't mess with me. Don't mislead me. You're testing me, I know you are, which I expected, but don't mess with me, it wasn't that tree, it was *that* tree there. You found a girl, a young girl, she died of her own stupid cause, her lifestyle, and that's where it was." Graff looked at him and said, "You're right. I'm not going to test you again dude. I don't know how you just did it, but even if you read about this crime in the newspaper that tree was never mentioned. And there's no way to tell anymore, that is, no physical markings." The "doubting Thomas," Graff then took Ward to another crime scene where Ward proceeded to recount in detail exactly how the crime occurred (see Chapter 6).

Other tests can easily be designed by the investigator with a little imagination. The psychics themselves can also be asked how their abilities may best be tested. Best results are often achieved if the psychics are allowed to take the tests home so they can work on them at their leisure and when they feel most receptive.

Precautions and Considerations

There are several precautions that should be observed during the testing phase. First of all, the cases used for testing purposes must be unknown to the psychics in order to prevent any contamination from information they may have picked up from the media. For this reason obscure or old cases should be used. Just because a case is old does not mean that it cannot be worked successfully with psychics. In fact, old unsolved cases are good ones to work on because there is nothing to lose since the investigation is at a dead end. Furthermore, they provide great experience for the psychic recruits. Some psychics claim that the "energy" of a crime event never really dissipates, especially in traumatic crimes, such as homicides. Other psychics believe that the spirit of the deceased hangs around the murder scene and can be contacted, even many years afterwards. Annette Martin is a case in point. Visiting a murder scene for the second time twenty years after the crime, she reexperienced the murder from the victim's point of view with the same intensity of years before. Similarly, she worked an unsolved thirty-five-year-old double homicide case in Montana and was instrumental in leading the detectives to the murderer, old and ill, in a hospital in California.

Second, the investigator must be careful not to give the psychics subtle clues as to the nature and circumstances of each case. This happens more easily than is generally believed through such cues as nods of approval, voice inflections, and leading and suggestive questions. Ideally, the testing should be *double-blind*, i.e., a neutral investigator assembles the packets and seals and numbers them so that the investigator testing the psychics does not know the nature of the cases. This precaution will theoretically rule out contamination through nonverbal behavior or possible telepathic transference from the investigator to the psychic. This can still present problems, however, as evidenced in one instance where the authors and Captain Wolverton were testing a new psychic. She was holding an envelope with some materials from a homicide case, but was giving detailed information about another case, a child molestation. Later that night Wolverton confided in us that all evening, and particularly at that specific moment, he had been thinking about a recent child molestation case he was working on and that the details were accurately described by the psychic. A similar instance involving another case led an FBI agent working with us to innocently state that he believed that the psychic was "merely reading my mind," not realizing that this was no small feat in itself.

It is also important to meet someplace where the psychic(s) is comfortable and relaxed, which usually means his or her home. The wrong place to work with them is at the police station. It is also important that the investigator keep the atmosphere light and the testing interesting. The psychics should not be made to feel that they are under pressure to perform, because the quality and quantity of information they obtain is often directly related to their degree of relaxation and receptivity. Experience throughout the world in ESP laboratories has shown clearly that psychic responses are also directly related to the novelty and interest factor of the test; if it's boring, the psychic performs less wel. Hence, it is important to use interesting testing procedures and material–and not to overtest.

It is important not to treat psychics as guinea pigs but as normal human beings generously giving their time and talent. To do otherwise will militate against successful testing. The extremes to which some scientists fail to do this was amply demonstrated when a famous trance medium known by the authors was asked by scientists studying him to go into trance with a rectal thermometer in place (for the purpose of monitoring physiological changes)!

Although it is convenient to conduct testing in small groups, and some psychics claim that the group "energy" helps them, there is certainly the potential problem of contamination, i.e., one psychic's responses influencing another's. For that reason alone, we believe that the most objective results are obtained from individual tests.

Before making the final determination of who is worth working with, the investigator should test each psychic using several different means on several different occasions. Experience has shown that any given psychic may be "on" or "off" on any particular day or may work well only on certain types of cases, such as missing persons.

Whatever tests the investigator uses, it is imperative to write down the recruits' responses and to objectively evaluate and score their performance. If significantly above chance, they are a keeper. If not, it's best to cull them out of the program. To do this, the investigator can simply thank them for their time, interest, and cooperation, then dismiss them on the pretest agreement that their continued participation in the project would hinge on the results.

METHODS OF PSYCHIC INVESTIGATION

Now that the investigator has identified, recruited, and tested the psychic recruits, he or she is ready to begin working with those who performed well on the tests. The major question to be answered at this point is how to work most effectively with the recruits?

Of primary importance is to convey to the psychic recruits the seriousness of your joint endeavor. Deputy Ferenc Zana of the King County Sheriff's Office, an experienced remote viewer, recommends impressing on your psychic informants that there are "real life ramifications" to their work, and that a case "is not a training opportunity where failure does not matter. You're not allowed to fail here. This has to be your frame of mind."

An initial concern will be whether to work with them individually or in a group. The authors have tried both, and there are advantages and disadvantages to each. The major advantage of working in a group is convenience; more information can be gained faster. The major disadvantage, as mentioned, is that there exists the important factor of group suggestion, i.e., one psychic will give his or her impressions, which may cue the others to follow with similar ones, especially if they consider that person more skilled than themselves. This clearly happened in one instance in which one of our groups was presented with the case of a missing teenager. The first psychic said that the teenager was alive, and all the rest followed suit. Over the next few months the group created endless fantasies about where he was and what he was doing. A new psychic was then brought into the group and asked what her impressions of the case were before she knew anything of what the group thought. She meditated a short while and said the teenager was dead by drowning and described in some detail the circumstances. Several months later his body was found in a lake.

An easy way of avoiding this verbal contamination in a group is simply to request silence until all group members have worked with the packet and received their impressions, *which they should write down.* When all are finished, the investigator can either collect what they have written (a sample form for their use is provided in the Appendix) or elicit their information verbally, which the investigator then writes down in his or her own manner. If the latter approach is used, it is important to take down exactly what the psychic says and avoid any interpretation or alteration of his or her own.

Another potential disadvantage of a group is the sense of competition between members, which may lead some to try to outdo themselves to try to impress the others. Another problem is that groups tend to quickly drift away from their *psychic impressions* to *theorizing* about the case. This is known as *analytical overlay* and occurs when a psychic attempts to analyze his or her intuitive responses intellectually. This tendency almost invariably produces errors. Some people are frustrated detectives, and if the investigator does not control the group and limit them to their psychic impressions, they will soon be trying to do the investigator's job. It is for this reason, as well as the fact that first impressions are usually the most accurate, that the investigator must repeatedly and periodically emphasize that only first impressions are of interest.

The advantage of working with psychics individually is that it solves the problems of suggestion and competition in one stroke, but it demands much more time of the investigator. It may be that only one or two of your recruits pass the testing phase, however, in which case there is no problem.

Although the tendency of the investigator when first working with psychics is to have them work on several important cases at once, experience has taught us that the best results will be obtained if they work only on one case per meeting. This way each meeting can begin afresh, and they will not confuse impressions from different cases, which often seems to be the case when working several cases simultaneously. The disadvantage of working only one case per meeting is that it may make for a very short meeting. If this is the case, the investigator can come prepared with some solved cases or other exercises previously mentioned in TESTING PSYCHICS for training purposes. It may be, however, that the investigator may have more than one pressing case that he or she feels should immediately be worked on by the group. In this instance, the investigator may be able to avoid contamination of impressions from one case to another if the group takes a ten- or fifteen- minute break between cases. In addition, the investigator should be certain that the case packets are individually wrapped and, preferably, carried separately to avoid mixing their "vibes." Several psychics have even insisted that each case packet be wrapped in tinfoil, explaining that it prevents any contamination.

An alternative and possibly superior procedure to meeting systematically is to pass out case material to each psychic and have them work it on their own time. They may then write down their impressions, which can be phoned in, mailed in, or picked up. This approach will take less of the investigator's time, and the psychics will have more freedom to work.

The investigator should prepare a case packet for each meeting, including similar items as described under testing Procedures. He or she should present each psychic with the material they request and let each work in his or her own way for the length of time they need. Depending on the requests from the group, the investigator may or may not tell them the nature of the crime, because some will want to know, and others will not. It should be clarified before the group starts active work on cases as to what kinds of cases the psychics are willing to work on, e.g., some will not want to work on violent crimes.

Another matter of concern is how much information to give the group. The authors experimented with telling the groups absolutely nothing, then only the type of crime and victim, then almost everything the police knew. We found that the less information we provided, the less we received; however, it was generally more accurate. The more background information we gave, the more we received, although it was less accurate and the psychics tended to theorize more. One advantage in giving more information was that the psychics could offer their impressions on specific pieces of evidence, clues, leads, suspects, and so forth.

The advantages of each approach can be gained by using a simple, three-step procedure. First, tell the group absolutely nothing about the crime, but let them handle the packet. Have each person record their impressions on the form provided. Second, tell the group the type of crime and the victim's name. Again, have each person record their impressions on the form. Third, tell the group everything you presently know through traditional investigation, then get their impressions on specific aspects, suspects, theories, etc. This technique will also give the investigator a continuous testing procedure by determining how accurate each psychic is by their responses on the first (blind) approach. In this way, the investigator can determine which psychics are on target on that particular day or case (some will have dry spells) and will also know how much credence to give the impressions received on steps two and three. For instance, if the investigator hands a packet to a psychic that contains items belonging to a missing girl and the psychic gets impressions of a bank robbery, it probably can be assumed that a good psychic connection has not been made. (However, it is possible, although unlikely, that the psychic may be picking up on the perpetrator's past criminal behavior.) On the other hand, if the psychic begins talking about the kidnapping of a girl, any additional information that isn't immediately verifiable must be given credence. In one case, for example, the body of a girl was found along a highway, but there were no clues as to her identity. The authors asked a reliable psychic for impressions. She went into a deep state of self-hypnosis and then reported that she could see that the girl was about sixteen years old, with brown hair, and had died of a drug overdose. No specific information of this nature had been released by the authorities. She then described the nature of her death and gave clues to her identity. Four days later the autopsy results revealed the girl was between fifteen and eighteen years old with brown hair, and her blood contained almost twice the lethal dose of pentobarbital. In this case, a great deal of credibility was given to the rest of the information provided by this psychic.

As during the testing procedure, it remains important for the investigator to be careful that he or she does not ask leading and suggestive questions, e.g., instead of asking, "Was the motive robbery?" noncommittally ask, "What was the motive?" Or when handing an object to a psychic to be psychometrized, the investigator should ask, "What can you tell me about this object?" or "What can you tell me about the person who this object belongs to?" instead of initially providing descriptive information around which anyone could create a story. In addition, the investigator should always retain some control questions to be asked periodically to gauge accuracy, i.e., case-related questions with known answers. At all times, he or she should be careful not to convey personal beliefs and biases regarding the case, because the psychics may subconsciously pick these up and feed them back as "impressions." When this occurs, the psychic is inadvertently telling the investigator exactly what he or she might want to hear, which may be entirely false. Dr. Truzzi believes that this is a persistent problem in psychic investigations and that some psychics' gift actually "may be one of unconscious pattern recognition and what is now termed implicit learning and tacit knowledge."

During the first part of each meeting the investigator should give the psychics feedback about the accuracy of the material provided the previous weeks. Usually this is not as easy as it sounds. Experience has shown that much of the information provided is of such a nature that it cannot be either verified or rejected through follow-up investigation. Until the case is actually solved, most of the information remains plausible and possibly true, but until an arrest is made, it cannot be evaluated fairly. For example, in the previously cited case of the drowned teenager, all the impressions of his current activity were plausible but unprovable until the body was found. Feedback remains important, however, because it helps the psychics evaluate their own performance and whether they are on the right track.

In addition to using such items as the victim's photograph, clothing, physical evidence, and crime scene photos as aids for plugging the psychics into the case, other things such as aerial photos, maps, lists, and mugshots of suspects are often helpful. Some psychics are able to accurately psychometrize or dowse maps and aerial photos. Several well-known psychics who specialize in psychic archaeology repeatedly and accurately locate buried artifacts, giving the exact location, depth, type, and age of the artifacts, just from looking at contour maps and aerial photos.

A unique ability demonstrated by some psychics is their capability for actually seeing a perpetrator's face. These rare psychics are able to provide a detailed physical description of the perpetrator and should be used in conjunction with a police artist or Identi-Kit®. In one reported case a police artist from San Jose, California, was sent to a Nevada hospital to interview a young girl who had been raped and mutilated. Even though the girl was just out of surgery and still in shock, the artist sat down beside her and started to get flashes of her assailant. He was able to draw a composite, which was published in the newspaper. The suspect's neighbor recognized the picture and gave the police his name, and he was subsequently arrested and convicted. The same police artist was sent to get a composite from a deaf mute who had been raped. Sitting beside her, he drew the composite from psychic images while she excitedly nodded her approval. A police officer recognized the composite and arrested the man. In another reported case, a retired policeman-turned-hypnotist, hypnotized and regressed a psychic to the day of the disappearance of a seven-year-old boy. The psychic described the face of a man she believed kidnapped the boy and described him to a police artist. The sketch was shown to the parents, who recognized the man as the person who worked on their automobiles. The man was arrested; he confessed to molesting and murdering the boy and two other boys and was sentenced to death. In a similar case in southern California, a police artist's drawing based on a psychic's description resulted in the arrest and conviction of a murderer.

A strong temptation for the investigator is to have the group or individuals work on the major unsolved cases over and over again. This is generally not recommended, because research and experience have shown that a psychic's first impressions are the best. Hence, the longer they work on a case, the more likely they are to become inaccurate. One detective, after several years of intensive work with psychics, finally came to the conclusion that the only psychic information worth paying attention to was that which came unsolicited and spontaneously. As new evidence and leads are developed, these could be presented to the psychics to help determine relative merit, meaning, and importance. The new evidence may also trigger psychic responses that were not available before. There will be exceptions to this basic "first impressions are best" rule, because some psychics take a long time to "warm up" to a case. They may literally have to sleep on it for some period of time, handle the material on different occasions, and even visit and revisit the crime scene before 'tuning in" to the case. This psychic differential is determined on an individual basis.

Often one of the most effective procedures of psychic investigation is to go on-site. This often greatly facilitates the intensity, quality, and quantity of impressions obtained from many psychics. Taking psychics to the scene of a violent crime is not without its risks, however. Many psychics so closely identify with the victim that they literally feel the victim's pain and often relive the crime itself to some extent. Most experienced psychics have learned to dissociate from another's pain, yet there are those who cannot. With the former there is no problem with taking them on-site if they think it will help, but with the latter extreme caution should be used. The investigator must always put the health and well-being of the psychics above the desire for more and better information. Those who are likely to experience trauma on a violent crime scene (most will have a good idea of how they may react beforehand) should not be taken. If they insist or want to try it anyway, approach the crime scene slowly, periodically ask the person how she or he is feeling, and observe any stress signs and manifestations of anxiety. If any are observed, the investigator should attempt to calm the subject with verbal reassurance and perhaps take him or her away from the scene.

The authors accompanied Det. Sgt. Keaton and an untested psychic to a mountainous area in California where a killer preyed on people hiking the trails. Suddenly the psychic, who was in the lead, ran down off the trail about thirty yards and got very excited and animated, speaking about how he believed the crime happened. He became increasingly involved in his scenario until he fell down and began pleading for his life. At this point we realized that he had identified with the victim and was apparently reliving her experience. We immediately went to his side and established physical and verbal contact. When he had regained his composure, we walked him out of the area and took him home. Keaton told us later that the place where the psychic "relived" the crime was one of the exact murder scenes. Keaton was understandably anxious to proceed, but the welfare of the psychic was the major priority.

In another instance, an FBI agent and a captain of detectives for the local sheriff's office took five special psychics out to a secluded, mountainous crime scene. Two of the psychics began to get agitated, one of whom was a new, untested recruit to the group. When on-site, the agent tried to organize the group, but each scurried off in separate directions. The two agitated members of the group seemed to key in to the violence of the place and became very hostile and combative. As the agent was trying to calm them, the other three were off by themselves. Because this was the captain's first experience with psychics, he did not know what to do and stood by the sidelines watching. As a result, little information was obtained, and a potentially bad experience with the two psychics was narrowly avoided. Looking back on the experience, the agent realized that he should not have taken so many at once—and especially not the one new psychic with whom he had no prior experience.

Although it has its risks as just illustrated, we believe that taking psychics to actual crime scenes maximizes the chances of psychic informants really tuning in to a particular case. Many psychics explain that they work on a "vibrational level," so it stands to reason to get them as close to the actual vibration of a crime as possible. Hence, the emphasis is on using actual physical evidence (e.g., blood-stained clothing, crime scene photos) or to take them on-site.

Interestingly, many psychics seem to work well at a distance. As a case in point, a district attorney in Lancaster County, Pennsylvania, asked the Mobius Society—a parapsychological research group in Los Angeles—to work on the case of a missing girl. Working only from a photograph, Mobius correctly described the location of the girl's body in a wooded area, the cause of death, and the background of her killer. According to the DA, "While I can't say they broke the case, they were very on target. We could have saved weeks of digging [in a landfill] had we had the faith and vision to interpret [their] statements."

An intriguing possibility of psychic investigation is to apply it proactively. Generally, this takes the form of patrol officers acting on gut feelings and hunches. Countless times we have heard patrol officers say, "I knew that was going to go down last night," and, "If only I'd paid attention to my gut feeling about sitting on that building a little longer. . . ." One officer on a proactive burglary-theft team—the Crime Attack Team in Missoula, Montana, co-directed by the authors (WH & RW)—spent several hours sitting and watching a building on the basis of a feeling that it was going to be hit. As time passed his rationality won out and he left; a few minutes later the building was burglarized. To this officer's later regret, he explained his feeling away at the time by thinking it illogical. Impressed by the frequency of these events, we continually urge officers to pay attention and react to their gut feelings and hunches instead of dismissing them. After all, reacting on the basis of a gut feeling or hunch is just as valid, if not more so, we believe, than random patrolling. Whether gut feelings and hunches are simply subconscious nudges based on computations of past experience for likely probabilities of events to come or extrasensory "leaks" is open to debate. Whether officers "accidentally" happen to be in the right place at the right time or are actually "guided" there is similarly debatable. One thing is for sure, however, and that is the fact that it is not unusual for a police officer to have a highly developed sixth sense. After all, they exercise it everyday on the job, constantly alert, looking, hunting, evaluating, and otherwise inadvertently developing their intuition and survival instinct.

One particularly gifted patrol officer had the unique ability to sense the presence of drugs and contraband in automobiles. When on patrol and working radar, he would psychically "read" each passing car, stopping and searching any that triggered his "psychic radar" (this was in the days and in a state in which this was legal). His sensing proved uncannily correct. Interestingly, no one in the department knew about his psychic talent. It was generally assumed that the officer's extremely high rate of arrests for possession of dangerous drugs and possession of stolen property was either luck or caused by the unlikely fact that a disproportionately large percentage of motorists carried drugs and stolen property in their cars.

A similar ability was demonstrated to the authors and two detectives by a psychic visiting from out of state. At his request the officers provided him with a plastic bag containing marijuana from the evidence locker. We got into a cruiser and began randomly patrolling streets. The psychic held the bag in one hand and put his other hand against the window. He explained that when we passed any house with a sizable amount of marijuana in it, he would feel a shock in his hand. We all kind of winked at each other thinking that this would be quite interesting. All of a sudden the psychic let out a yell and jerked his hand away from the window and pointed to a house exclaiming, "That's it!" The two detectives glanced unbelievingly at each other and said almost in unison that that house belonged to the biggest drug dealer in town. The psychic found one other hot spot in an open lot. Again, the surprised detectives said that they had recovered a cache of marijuana there.

On rare occasions, psychic information has enabled the police to successfully intervene in criminal activity. In one instance, a manager of a restaurant asked a psychic friend in another state for a personal reading. As part of the reading, the psychic saw her friend somehow involved with a thief. This interested the manager, because her restaurant had been burglarized twice, and she was already having a local psychic work with the police on the cases. The manager sent her psychic friend twenty-five personnel files, thinking that it was an inside job. Doing a separate reading on each file proved to be too laborious, so out of frustration the psychic suddenly asked, "Who did it?" She described what happened next as "seeing globally." She suddenly saw the images of three people planning a burglary, including a young man, his girlfriend, and another man. She could hear their conversation, which centered around the first man, who admitted to burglarizing the restaurant the first two times. The psychic called the manager and provided her with the information, including a description of the burglar. The manager passed the information on to the police. Fortunately, the police felt confident enough of the information to stake out the restaurant that night. The burglar struck that night and was arrested. He closely matched the description provided by the psychic. Interestingly, the psychic had also said that the burglar was hired to pull the jobs by an enemy of the restaurant owner, and that if he were released on bail, he would be killed. The burglar was released on bail and has not been seen since.

Occasionally an officer or a citizen will intuitively know who committed a certain crime. In one instance a young married woman whose car was broken into and the tape deck stolen intuitively *knew* who was responsible. She drove downtown, parked, and waited for four black men in a blue Mustang (how she knew this she didn't know or care). In a short while along came a blue Mustang with four black men in it. The car parked, the men got out, and they started going up the street with a clothes hanger looking for cars to break into. She took the license plate number and called the police. They responded and arrested the men. She did not retrieve her tape deck, because it had already been fenced. On another occasion her tape deck was stolen again out of her car. Like the first time, she intuitively *knew* who took it (even though she did not personally know the person responsible), so she stole it back. There was no doubt that it was her tape deck because her name was on it.

Another important, although less frequent, aspect of using psychic experiences proactively is dreams—the reader is reminded of the story in Chapter 1 in which an officer could have saved his own life if he had acted on his own dream. A similar instance involved another officer in his prelaw enforcement days. While at sea on a naval aircraft carrier, he had an extremely vivid, multicolored dream in which he saw a downed pilot float by the ship, unconscious, and supported by his life vest. Interestingly, he even backed the dream up and saw it happen over again three times. The dream was so real and lifelike that it was disconcerting and awakened him. The next day while on deck a plane powered-out on takeoff, the pilot ejected (the force of which knocked him unconscious), and he floated by the ship exactly as seen in the dream. The pilot inadvertently ended up being killed by the rescue team through a tragedy of errors, and to this day the officer has a nagging feeling that his precognitive dream may have been an indication for him to dive in after the pilot and save him, an urge that he had at the time.

On only one other occasion since that event has this particular officer had such a vivid dream. This dream happened when he was a peace officer. In the dream he walks through the front door of a house to serve a warrant and finds the man sitting in a rocking chair with a blanket over his lap. Suddenly he throws the blanket aside and comes up with a gun, at which point the dream ends. The officer, needless to say, is watching and waiting for this particular event. He believes that if he recognizes the situation before it happens, he will have a split-second advantage, thus saving his own life.

A precognitive dream of another police officer was reported in the files of Dr. J. B. Rhine at Duke University. One morning at 4 A.M. an insurance investigator was awakened by his friend, the police officer, who asked to borrow his .44 Smith & Wesson revolver. Without explanation the officer handed over his Colt .38 with the warning not to carry it. At 10 A.M. the insurance investigator received a call from the officer who was in the hospital. The officer had walked into a holdup, killed two of the robbers and wounded a third, having shot five rounds with the borrowed .44 before being hit in the chest. When the officer's Colt .38 was later test-fired, the mainspring failed on the third shot. When the officer was told the results he showed no surprise, explaining that he had dreamt he was in a shootout and that his gun failed on the third shot.

Other dream experiences show a mixture of precognitive and retrocognitive aspects. A paramedic, a personal friend of the authors, was asleep in his bed at the ambulance station. While asleep, he had a vivid dream that a man knocked on the window of his partner's room and then crawled in bed with him. The dream was so realistic that he felt compelled to get up and check on his partner. As he was doing so, they were dispatched to render medical assistance to a man who had severely cut his wrist. He had broken out a window in a house, gained entry, crawled in bed with a woman, and raped her. According to the paramedic's best estimate, his dream had to have occurred five to ten minutes *after* the man cut his hand, yet immediately *before* receiving the call.

Dreams seem to be the most frequent means of paranormally obtaining information in nonpsychic people. Several authenticated cases have been reported by the Society for Psychical Research of dreams of murders and dreams of the solutions to murders, usually by close friends or relatives of the victims.

Not all precognition experiences occur in dreams. Some occur to people in their normal waking state. Sometimes the experiences are heard or seen, or the person just has a vague sense of knowing. The following experience reported of Sir Winston Churchill is typical:

> This has to do with his habit of going out to boost the morale of London's civil defense forces at night in a car during the air raids of World War II. This night the driver held the near-side door open for him, as he always sat on the near side. But when he got to the open door, he stopped, went round to the off-side, opened the off-side door, got in and sat on the off-side. He had never done this before. He told the driver to start, so the driver closed the near-side door and they proceeded to drive along the Kingston bypass at 60 miles per hour. Suddenly a bomb fell near the off-side of the car, and the force of the explosion lifted it up onto the near-side wheels. However, before somersaulting right over, the car righted itself and sped on. At 60 mph it is very probable that if it had gone over, both Churchill and the driver would have been killed. "That was a near one," joked Winston. "It must have been my beef on this off-side that brought the car back down."

> He did not tell his wife so as not to scare her, but she heard about it from the driver and decided to challenge him about the incident. "Winston, why did you get in on the off-side of the car?" "I don't know, I don't know," Winston answered at first, but his wife pierced him with her gaze and he realized he could not get away with that answer, so he said, "Yes I do know. When I got to the near-side door held open for me, something in me said 'Stop, go round to the other side and get in there,' and that is what I did."

A similar instance is reported by Dr. Louisa Rhine of the Foundation for Research on the Nature of Man (formerly the Duke University Parapsychology Laboratory):

> A mother had a waking picture of her eldest son, Herbert, dead in the bathtub. It haunted her so that she made a special point of listening that nothing went wrong, but she did not tell him her impression although she told her younger son, Peter. After a couple of years Herbert went away and when he came home for a holiday she still remembered it. One

evening on this visit she heard him whistling and singing in the bathtub. She was dressed to go out, but could not leave. After a while she heard the water running out but did not hear him singing so she opened the door, and there he lay exactly as she had seen him two years before. There was gas heat and the window was closed, and he had apparently been overcome by fumes. She immediately opened the door and windows and called the doctor and he was revived. If she had not been there, he doubtless would have died.

Dr. Rhine has reported another case of precognition that resulted in a successful intervention:

> It concerns a mother who dreamed that in two hours a violent storm would loosen a heavy chandelier to fall directly on her baby's head lying in a crib below it; in the dream she saw her baby killed. She awoke her husband who said it was a silly dream and that she should go back to sleep as he then did. The weather was so calm that the dream did appear ridiculous and she could have gone back to sleep. But she did not. She went and brought the baby back to her own bed. Two hours later, just at the time she specified, a storm caused the heavy light fixture to fall right where the baby's head had been.

A young mother known personally to the authors was asleep in bed when all of a sudden for no apparent reason, she woke up, jumped out of bed, and darted into her baby's room just in time to catch a large humidifier in mid-air as it was falling off its table on top of the baby.

The interesting and important aspect of these last four stories is that the premonition, and the crucial element of paying attention to it and acting on it, allowed for successful intervention. An analysis of thousands of premonitions has shown that between one third to one half of them could have been acted on to prevent disaster. Such premonitions by credible and proven psychics, then, can obviously be an aid to proactively oriented law enforcement agencies. It is instructive to note that there are on record three cases in which parapsychologists died accidental deaths by not heeding the premonitions of psychics working with them.

There is an inherent irony in trying to prove the accuracy of psychic warnings, because if a crime is prevented from occurring because of evasive or corrective action, it is impossible to say with certainty that the crime would have happened as predicted.

Premonitions are not unusual and are experienced by most people at one time or another. If experienced by a peace officer, they should be heeded. Consider the experiences related in Chapter 1 of the officers killed on duty.

Another psychic ability that is a valuable aid to interrogation is the capacity to see auras. The authors know several detectives and a polygraph examiner who claim to see auras. During an interrogation of a suspect, they can determine whether he or she is telling the truth because their aura shrinks at the point of lying. The polygrapher has been able to correlate this observation with his polygraph machine.

In exploring this new investigative tool, the investigator must be careful not to expect too much, because the results often will be equivocal. He or she must at the outset be determined to give it a fair shake, realizing that psychic investigation will likewise be new to the recruits; all concerned will be feeling their way and learning how to work best. Often a considerable amount of experimentation is necessary to determine such things as: exactly what types of cases each psychic works with best, what types of information or case-related items are needed to plug each psychic into the case, and what psychic aids or tools are best for each, e.g., meditation, psychometry, self-, or group hypnosis. The officer must also guard against the strong temptation to dismiss the whole project at the first failure, which is especially likely if he or she is overly skeptical.

A potential problem faces the investigator if the psychics work on cases for which he or she does not have investigative responsibility. If the other investigators are not aware of the project, he or she may have difficulty explaining the source of information. Even if the other investigators are aware of the project, they may not be sympathetic to it. In either case, it may be difficult to motivate the respective detectives to do the necessary follow-up. In this event, the investigator should seek their permission to follow up the psychic leads personally. To avoid this situation, the project officer may seek prior consent and enlist the support of the various case investigators on the cases that he or she wants to pursue. Another option is for the project officer to only work on cases for which he or she has personal responsibility. Yet another option is to work primarily on major unsolved cases that have been filed.

A good line of argument to be taken with the reluctant investigator is illustrated in the following story. The authors approached a captain of detectives with the idea of trying psychics on one of the department's unsolved homicides. He was not particularly enthusiastic about the prospect, yet at this point in the case he had nothing to lose and was willing to try anything. With the captain's help, we put together a packet of case items and sent it off to Beverly Jaegers' U.S. PSI Squad. A few weeks later we received a written synopsis of two typed pages, which we presented to the captain. He quickly scanned the material and announced, "Well, this isn't correct because we know from the physical evidence that the murderer came in the front door and it says here that he came in the back door. And it says here that she was sitting in the kitchen drinking tea, but I known that she didn't drink tea." A little discouraged, we waited in anticipation while he resumed reading from the beginning, stopping occasionally to think, then re-reading for a few minutes, during which time his facial expression became steadily more serious and interested. After what seemed like an eternity, he finally put the paper down, leaned back in his chair, took off his glasses, gazed at the ceiling, and said, "You know, come to think of it, it does make more sense that he came in the back door instead of the front. There always was something about that crime-scene that bothered me." At this point he literally jumped up, strode to the file cabinet, and returned with an envelope full of crime scene photos and a floor plan of the victim's house. He soon came to a photo and paused, looked up at us in disbelief, and handed us the picture. It was a picture of the kitchen and there on the kitchen table was a teapot! After a few minutes of reflection, the captain made the following insightful statement that is the lesson of this story: "You know, I really don't care where this information comes from or how they get it, and it really doesn't matter if it's true or false, but the important thing is that it forces me to look at a case in a new light."

It is this exact reasoning that is most effective with the reluctant and skeptical investigator. Psychically obtained information may in many cases be no more valid than any other kind, but the important factor is that it stimulates new and different perspectives from which to reevaluate evidence, as well as one's own predilections and conclusions.

Another technique for mollifying, or even gaining, the active support of an entire detective division is to arrange for an orientation lecture and possibly a demonstration by either a credible expert or author on ESP and the paranormal, a well-known psychic, or even a persuasive and talented member of your group. The authors tested this approach on our first attempt at introducing psychic investigation to a local police department and sheriff's office with whom we were working as coordinators of a special crime control project. At considerable risk to our own credibility, we flew in a Ph.D. who had just written a book on psychic archaeology. We called a general meeting of the detective divisions from both departments with the simple explanation that we had flown in an expert on some new investigative procedure. The fact that we would not give any further information, even after considerable prodding, only heightened the anticipation and increased attendance. At the meeting we introduced the doctor and displayed his book, which established his authority. He then proceeded to discuss his experiences with our skeptical, captive audience regarding his successful use of psychics in archaeology and how it could be applied to criminology. By the end of the hour most of the audience were enthusiastic believers and were demanding that we arrange for training so they could develop their own latent psychic abilities!

Chapter 5

WORKING WITH PSYCHICS

In working with psychics in investigations, there are numerous considerations, precautions, and potential problems for which the investigator should be prepared.

Most investigators quickly discover that there is a language and conceptual barrier between themselves and their psychics. Psychics often use a specialized vocabulary derived from their different worldviews and conceptions of reality. Although at first, most psychics are cautious and play the straight and narrow, they soon loosen up as mutual trust and rapport builds. They might then begin speaking of strange things in unfamiliar terms. Some psychics intentionally do this to test the investigator, i.e., to elicit his or her beliefs. This gives the psychic a feel for how much he or she can open up. In this regard, it is important for the investigator to be open-minded and not outwardly reject anything that the psychics say; after all, in this domain the psychic is the expert, the investigator the novice. The investigator should, however, ask for explanations of terms and ideas that are unfamiliar or else he or she may soon feel lost. For example, it is common for psychics to talk about "channeling" information from their "guides." This one sentence introduces the uninitiated to several new words and concepts, including a novel means of receiving information from nonhuman beings existing in realms other than our known physical one. The Glossary will familiarize the reader with some often-used terms.

Exposure to a novel conception of reality in which most psychics firmly believe (in one form or another) can be disconcerting to the investigator; it presents a challenge to one's taken-for-granted worldview. Exposure to the paranormal can force one to seriously question one's own view of reality and what one has unquestioningly assumed

80

to be true. The investigator may soon discover that, to the psychic, the world is more than it seems; there are many levels of reality (only some of which are perceived by the five senses); consciousness or mind is separate from the brain, not confined to the physical body, and does not die at physical death; and nonphysical beings interpenetrate our world and can communicate with the human mind, to name a few.

The investigator may find all this confusing, ludicrous, imaginary, disturbing, possibly true or exciting; a host of reactions may be stimulated. Deputy Zana, for example, admits to having his life radically changed by his exposure to remote viewing which stimulated an intense training period of learning how to do it himself. The authors recommend that the investigator maintain a healthy skepticism, constantly remember the purpose of the project, and not be particularly concerned about the whys or hows of psychic phenomena. In the final analysis, it's really a question of usefulness; if it works, use it. If the authors' experience can serve as a gauge, after one's initial skepticism is overcome, the investigator can expect to become enthralled, even enchanted, with the psychics and their worldviews. "Its mystique," cautions Chief Kozenczak (ret.), "once experienced, may become addictive." The once skeptical investigator may become a firm believer. A typical example is an officer who worked on the John Wayne Gacy case, who said in reference to a female psychic the department used, "Either this woman killed the guy or there's really something to this psychic stuff!"

With experience, however, the investigator may become jaded. After dealing with dozens of psychics intimately, the authors reached a point where we saw and heard about everything; nothing surprises us anymore. This has proven to be an advantageous state of mind, because new psychics quickly recognize that we know where they are coming from, hence a mutual understanding, rapport, and working relationship are established more quickly.

Many people like to impose their beliefs on others, and psychics are no different. Although most psychics that we have dealt with have been respectful of our personal views and beliefs, there are always those suffering from the "missionary disease," which is the overwhelming impulse to preach and convert others to one's personal worldview. How the officer deals with this is an individual matter. The authors recommend that the investigator remain understanding but firm in the reinforcement of the basic purpose, ground rules, and objectives of the relationship; in other words, to get results.

Sometimes a psychic will want to train the officer in certain psychic abilities and tools. Again, this is an individual matter for the officer and should present no problem as long as he or she continues to pursue the project's original goal in the predetermined manner. In fact, some proponents suggest that law enforcement officers should be trained in psychic investigation, thereby avoiding the potential problems and pitfalls of working with lay psychics outside the department. A few departments, such as the Pomona Police Department in California, made initial forays into this uncharted territory with the aid of outside consultants, like Dr. Ludwig's PsiCom. At present, a few law enforcement agencies are having some of their officers trained in remote viewing by consultants such as Buchanan, who argues for this type of in-house training:

> It is my feeling that an investigator knows the needs of investigative work better than does a housewife or shoe salesman. They know what to look for, how to report it in official and acceptable police jargon, etc. Therefore, you should train investigators to be their own "controlled remote viewers" [a special form of RV]. They are much better suited for the job than anyone else. Those departments who have come to me and formed a controlled remote viewing group within their department continue to use their personnel as controlled remote viewers, and have reported (to me, at least), quite a bit of success. In fact, their success rate appears to be higher than when they work with even better trained controlled remote viewers through the Assigned Witness Program. When someone who is trained leaves their department, they send another officer to train as a replacement. We have had very few departments which are willing to do this, but those which have have reported quite a great amount of success.

Close personal contact over a period of time with psychics, as with anyone, presents potential problems. The investigator will quite naturally develop likes and dislikes for each, and the tendency will be to give more credence to the information provided by those liked and to disregard information from those disliked. This is a mistake, because there is no apparent correlation between personality and the quality of information received. It may be that the psychic liked least may provide the best information. The investigator must be careful, therefore, to give equal consideration and follow-up to all the information obtained from everyone.

In addition to the strong tendency to pick and choose which information to follow up, there is an equally strong tendency to interpret the information according to the investigator's preconceptions. It is in the act of interpretation that lies the ever-present possibility of misinterpretation. It is extremely important for the investigator to record and act on the psychic information exactly as it is given instead of trying to conform it to some preconception about the crime. This is especially important if information is being passed on to other investigators.

A case in point occurred several years ago when the authors had a psychic do a reading on a missing girl. Although the psychic had never been to the community in which the girl was missing, she said the girl would be found in an area where there were two Quonset® huts, that there was "something to do with garbage," and a place where people parked. She also saw a log house within sight of the body, a large red tank, and a large pipe or pipes as if there was something like a pumping station. She also said she saw a "Bean" or "B Mountain," that the site was near a road that left town and went to higher ground, that the road went by a water tower, and her body would be found around the middle of the next month. Unfortunately, we did not send the notes directly to the sheriff's office but relayed the information by telephone, adding that it sounded as if she may be referring to a rest stop on the highway or an oil field pumping station. Armed with this information, the sheriff's office assembled a group of deputies, city police, and highway patrol officers and searched all rest areas and pumping stations. The body was found the middle of the following month as predicted after some kids found the girl's scarf. The body was found in a ravine below an old city sewage pump house, which had a large sewer drainpipe coming out of one end. There was a red gasoline tank for filling the city vehicles, city garbage trucks were parked there, three Quonset® huts were in view, and a log house belonging to the undersheriff was on a distant hill overlooking the site. In addition, the teenager's lover's lane was on the bluff above the ravine, a road went through the area to higher ground, two water towers were nearby, and the city letters "CB" were on a hill directly across from the location. Interestingly, the B was more prominent than the C. In retrospect, the investigating deputies were convinced that they could have gone directly to the site had they had the original notes. Because of our particular interpretation, however, and not sending the notes to the sheriff's office, the officers spent a great deal of time and effort searching rest areas and oil field pumping stations.

Other potential problems include the following: (1) some psychics may become too enthusiastic to the point of calling the investigator often with new information, (2) some may want further legitimacy by being deputized, (3) some may develop a sexual attraction to the investigator (or vice versa), and (4) the investigator may become a counselor for a psychic's personal problems (or vice versa). All such potential problems will have to be dealt with individually as perceived by the investigator. He or she should always keep foremost in mind, however, the objectives and integrity of the project and the department.

Some psychics will intensely experience the crime being worked on, so the investigator should be prepared for some seemingly bizarre behavior and have some idea how to deal with it. In one instance, the authors were recruiting a woman who had a good reputation as a psychic in the community. Sitting in the living room casually talking with her and her husband, we mentioned a recent homicide in which a man had been shot in the chest with a big-game rifle. As soon as she began to concentrate on the case, she grabbed her chest with both hands and crumpled to the floor screaming, "It hurts, it burns, it burns!" At this point, we knelt beside her, established physical contact, and began to talk her down in the following manner: "Now listen to me. Just relax, take a deep breath, and start to bring yourself back. Leave the crime scene and the victim. Don't identify with the victim and the pain; there's no need for you to do that. Now straighten your legs out and bring your hands down to your side as you listen to me, leave the pain and the victim, and come back to being fully with all of us in this living room. That's it, you're doing fine." Once she had regained her normal consciousness, we had her stand up and walk around outside in the fresh air. Then we discussed her experience. From her perspective she *was* the victim and felt his pain. To protect her both mentally and physically it was important to establish physical and verbal contact to try to ground her in her present waking reality and break her identification with her psychic experience. It was also important to then spend some time with her (and her husband who was watching helplessly!) until she had completely regained her normal consciousness. A follow-up phone call the next day was also important to make sure she wasn't having further difficulty.

In other instances, we've had psychics see ectoplasmic manifestations of victims, go into various trance states, perform automatic writing, and manifest physiological reactions of shivering, headaches, nausea, and hot flashes. Other psychics perform little rituals that supposedly aid their receptivity, such as meditation, self-hypnosis, prayers, and holding hands in a circle. Techniques used may include readings from ordinary playing cards or tarot cards, psychometry, horary astrology, I Ching, trance states, pendulum, and dowsing. All of these psychic tools can be effective. To illustrate, we will relate an experience with *horary*, which is a form of astrology designed for the purpose of answering specific questions.

Our introduction to horary was from an older and very successful businesswoman, who has proven to be one of our best "psychic" informants (she insists that astrology is an exact science that uses precise mathematical calculations and that there is nothing "psychic" about it). She first became interested in horary when an astrologer friend visited her and her husband in 1945. The astrologer did a natal horoscope on each and told the wife that her husband should watch his health carefully. A few years later he died of a cerebral hemorrhage. Out of curiosity the wife dug out the horoscope, turned it over, and there in black and white it said that her husband would die of a cerebral hemorrhage. This sparked her intense interest and study in horary. As a typical example of the results that can be obtained with this technique, a detective asked her for the status and location of a missing person. A retarded man in his forties was missing during the winter from the Montana ranch he lived on. A dog master was dispatched from the state police dog training academy. He searched the area without success. That night the astrologer completed her calculations and told the detective that the body would be found 1½ miles west of the ranch by an old slaughterhouse. The detective phoned this information to the dog master who said that there was no slaughterhouse around there. The next day, the dog master asked the rancher about an old building foundation he saw about 1½ miles west and he said, "Oh, that was an old slaughterhouse." The body was found later on a small ridge in the immediate vicinity.

The same horary astrologer was asked to do a chart on a young woman who was last seen at a laundromat in a small western town. The astrologer said that her body would be found twenty-six miles to the northeast in water. It was found twenty miles directly north then six miles directly east under a bridge over a large river.

Psychometry and map dowsing can also be very effective as evidenced in the following case. In 1975, an ex-convict murdered a young woman and disappeared. A professional "psychic counselor" came into the investigating sheriff's office and volunteered some information. Using maps to dowse and personal belongings of the suspect to psychometrize, the psychic said that the perpetrator went to the Seattle area where he would be found. She also said that he would be wearing white clothing as part of his job and would kill again. Exactly one year later, the suspect was located in the Seattle area where he was working in a convalescent hospital and wearing a white uniform. He was arrested for attempted murder after stabbing a seventeen-year-old girl. Left for dead in the woods, she survived and identified her assailant. The psychic also told the detectives what type of ID the suspect would be using under an assumed name. This was later confirmed.

The same psychic counselor was asked to psychometrize the clothes of a young woman who had been stabbed multiple times with an ice pick, set on fire, and then shot. With no prior knowledge of the case, the psychic said the victim was burned, stabbed with what looked like a needle-type instrument, and that there was a gunshot. As Det. Sgt. Keaton believes, "The use of psychometry is outstanding and a helluva tool."

Another psychic, using map dowsing, pinpointed a location where she believed the body of a missing man would be found. When the body was eventually found, she proved to be precisely correct, even though she lived in another state and was totally unfamiliar with the area.

There are some psychic tools that should be approached with caution. In particular is the séances. By some accounts, the drama of the séance draws many charlatans, magicians, and showmen. Critics have a heyday debunking and exposing phony mediums—of which there are many—yet they are hard pressed to explain how some accurately imitate the personality and speech patterns of unknown people and provide information known only to those close to the deceased.

Séances made their entry onto the modern social scene along with the birth of spiritualism in the mid-1800s, when Charles B. Rosma, a murder victim, began to communicate by means of rappings to the famous Fox sisters in Hydesville, New York. By rapping out "yes" or "no" answers to questions, he provided the details of his death and the location of his body, all of which later proved to be accurate. The rapping phenomenon as a technique of spirit communication later evolved into trance communication around a table with a medium.

In one well-documented case, a medium was consulted regarding the murder of a seventeen-year-old girl. The medium went into a trance, and her voice changed to that of a young woman, who identified herself as the murdered girl. The voice accurately described her manner of death, her two murderers, and said that they were presently sitting in a bar. She gave the name of the bar and the town. This information was passed on to the police who later arrested two suspects identified by the bartender from the girl's descriptions.

An ex-police officer-turned-psychic related an incident to the authors in which his assistance was sought by the parents of a missing girl. He psychometrized some of her clothing and determined that she had been killed. He then conducted a séances during which the girl's "spirit" explained how she was murdered, named the killer, described his truck, and gave the location of her buried body. Armed with this information the police found the body, and another one, exactly where indicated, but were not able to prove that the man named committed the murders.

This same psychic, who describes himself as a "waking medium" (i.e., spiritually guided but does not use trance), was asked to locate the body of a young woman believed drowned. He walked to the water's edge where her clothes and jewelry had been found and suddenly exclaimed, "She's not dead! This is a hoax!" The missing woman appeared several hours later, confessing that she faked her disappearance as a result of a family disagreement.

Caution must be used even when dealing with genuine mediums, because there is no guarantee of the legitimacy of the "spirits" contacted. An assumption is often made that information provided by a "spirit" must be accurate, because they apparently have access to more information than we embodied humans do. This seems to be an unfounded belief, because there seem to be dummies, liars, and tricksters on the "other side," just as there are here. In fact, Edgar Cayce, the famous trance medium, once stated in response to those who wanted to try to contact him after his death that all they would get is Edgar Cayce. The implication was that they would get Cayce the man and not his phenomenal psychic source that he had access to during his life, and therefore they would be wasting their time.

Some psychics will refuse to work certain cases if they feel that the crimes occurred as a result of karmic debts; if so, it is not the province of the psychic to interfere, they believe. Such refusals should be respected by the investigator.

Investigators often become frustrated with psychic information. Their obvious hope is that a good psychic can tell exactly how a crime happened, the perpetrator's name, license plate number, and so forth. Unfortunately, this is seldom the case. Psychic information is usually incomplete, sporadic, sometimes symbolic, and often seemingly irrelevant. For example, a deputy sheriff called a nationally known psychic sleuth regarding a missing boy. Over the telephone, she said that she saw the numbers 93081, a cemetery, a yellow house with red trim, got the name of Roberts, and smelled a terrible odor. She also said that the boy had suffocated in mud. The psychic could not say what any of this information meant, so it was up to the deputy to decipher it. He reasoned that since Highway 93 went through the middle of the valley, he would go up to milepost 81. At milepost 81 there was a cemetery and nearby a yellow house with red trim. He also smelled a terrible odor from a pig farm close by. The deputy then realized that a young man had indeed suffocated after being thrown from his dune buggy, knocked unconscious, and landed face down in the mud. He later discovered that the man was buried by a Mr. Roberts, the funeral director, whose license number was 13-980. Unfortunately, the psychic apparently had tuned into another case.

Psychics seem to be most accurate in describing personality and physical characteristics of perpetrators. For instance, two psychics were asked about the perpetrator responsible for a series of homicides on the West coast. Independent of each other, both said the perpetrator had a speech impediment, and one said he had scars on his chest, as if from shrapnel, and had been in a mental institution. A few days after the readings, a suspect was arrested. He had a pronounced stutter, had two or three scars on his chest from being shot by a military policeman, and had been in a mental institution.

Very seldom are correct names given. On several occasions the authors have been given correct initials of suspects' first and last names, but on only one occasion was a psychic able to provide a detective the correct first names of his prime suspect and girlfriend. As it turned out, the detective cleared this particular suspect, but later arrested and convicted a man and his girlfriend with the same first names. In one dramatic case, Peter Hurkos, upon walking into the Sharon Tate mansion shortly after the murderous rampage by Charles Manson's group, said right then and there that "a guy named Charlie" was responsible. On occasion, when names are provided by psychics, the spelling may be phonetic; that is, the psychic may spell a name as it sounds, although it may not be the correct spelling.

Although it is very difficult to get correct names of people psychically, psychics sometimes get correct place names. For instance, a sheriff's department asked for assistance in locating a sixty-two-year-old rancher who had disappeared. After a few quick phone calls to several psychics around the country, a lot of information was obtained, including three names. One psychic said to search by a place called Wyman. As it turned out, there is an old homestead called the Wyman Place adjacent to the ranch, but this is only known by the old-timers. Another psychic said to look southwest of Knobs, but couldn't say what the significance of Knobs was. It was learned that Knobs is an old town that used to be a post office but is no longer there. And another psychic from a distant state said to look in the Cannonball River. There is in fact a Cannonball River in the area, but it is only shown on contour maps, which the psychic would not have access to on such short notice.

In a similar instance, a friend of Santa Fe police officer Dan Chappell was missing. The missing man's mother contacted psychic Annette Martin from California who came to Santa Fe. Martin took a photo of the missing man and put it in a tube on a divining rod. Chappell relates the following story:

> We went northwest of Santa Fe because we believed my friend was in an area called Diablo Canyon. Annette used her diving rod but it kept pointing to the east instead of Diablo Canyon, which was to the northwest. Annette told us that my friend was in an area called Diablo Canyon and was near water. We knew about Diablo Canyon but her diving rod kept pointing east. So we searched Diablo Canyon for a few days as it's near the Rio Grande. We didn't find anything and a few months later a jogger finds the body in the mountains to the east where Annette had indicated. The body was found not fifty feet from a huge water tank.

Chappell consulted an old Forest Service map that showed that in the 1950s the area in which the body was found had in fact been called Diablo Canyon. Martin's rod had pointed directly to it.

An additional problem is that most psychics cannot give an accurate time frame for their information, i.e., they often cannot tell if what they receive refers to the past, present, or future. For example, a psychic being driven around a county by the sheriff in search of a body said that she saw a boy drown in a swimming pool. The skeptical sheriff said, "I'm sorry, but there is no swimming pool in this area." The psychic replied firmly, "Well, that's what I see!" A few minutes later the sheriff exclaimed, "By God, there used to be a swimming pool right over there across the street! A boy drowned in it about twelve years ago, so they filled it in!"

Psychic readings are subject to several forms of interference, including: (1) confusing information regarding the perpetrator with the victim, (2) confusing impressions from different cases, (3) picking up impressions telepathically from the investigator, (4) intrusion of extraneous impressions having nothing to do with the case, and (5) "accretion," i.e., adding on impressions that are not related. If any of these forms of interference is suspected, simply suggest the possibility to the psychic and ask him or her to concentrate on the distinction. If notified when they are going astray, many psychics can bring themselves back on track. Such problems should impress on the investigator the need for continually measuring psychic impressions against facts already known and not blindly following them. It is always necessary to intelligently evaluate psychic information so that it doesn't lead the investigation astray and waste valuable man-hours. Remember that, as with the best investigator, the best psychic will make mistakes.

A major problem often encountered with psychics who have a particularly strong interest or belief in the existence of certain otherworldly dimensions, beings, or cults is that they tend to interpret cases in light of their beliefs and preconceptions like anyone else. For example, the authors were testing a potential psychic on some missing-person cases. In our casual conversation beforehand we discovered that he had strong beliefs in space beings ("space brothers" as he referred to them) and that seeing spaceships was a common occurrence for him. Not surprisingly, he said in response to each of the three cases that each person had been "beamed off the planet." Obviously, we chose to not work any further with this person.

A similar instance involved another potential psychic who was very interested in witchcraft covens and black magic cults, even professing the belief that they controlled the world by infiltrating the power structures of all countries. Not surprisingly, she saw each missing person as a sacrificial victim of cults. Obviously, we chose to not work any further with this person either.

Similarly, although several United States law enforcement agencies and the Royal Canadian Mounted Police in Alberta have evidence that at lease some of the cattle mutilations are being done by cults, the psychics we have had work on mutilation cases tended to see them in light of their particular beliefs. Those who believe in cults believe that cults are responsible. Bigfoot fans believe that bigfoot is culpable. Those who believe in extraterrestrials believe that they are doing it. Those who subscribe to conspiracy theories blame the government, and on and on.

The important lesson for the investigator is to be alert for such contamination from psychics' belief systems. He or she must learn to sort out—and continually urge the psychics to do likewise—the genuinely received psychic information from that which the psychic preconceives, fantasizes, or would *like* to believe. The investigator must realize that psychic impressions are filtered through the receiver's subconscious mind and may be slightly altered or confused with memories and beliefs in the process. It is helpful to periodically urge the psychics to make a continuous effort to prevent or sort out the interference. As with all informants, the wheat must be separated from the chaff.

Just as important as the psychic's belief system are the beliefs, attitudes, and expectations of the investigator. Research in the behavioral sciences has clearly demonstrated that the researcher often subconsciously and unknowingly influences the results. He or she subtly, albeit unknowingly, transmits an expectation of a certain result to the subject(s) through verbal and nonverbal cues. If he or she has a negative bias and anticipates failure of the experiment, the subject will often subconsciously pick this up and behave accordingly. Conversely, if the experimenter has a positive bias and anticipates the success of the experiment, this will unknowingly be transmitted to the subject who will fulfill the expectation. The implications for psychic investigation are clear: It is essential for success that the investigator have a positive attitude and expectation of success. In addition, he or she should have a genuine faith and confidence in the psychic's abilities. In essence, the investigator clearly needs to be on the psychic's side and rooting for success. If he or she cannot genuinely do this, failure is likely predetermined. For example, dowsers maintain that dowsing will work only if the dowser believes that it works. (Although probably true, this line of reasoning can be a convenient excuse for failure; that is, if a neophyte tries dowsing and it doesn't work, an experienced dowser may explain away the failure on the pretext that the neophyte really doesn't believe in it. In a field as nebulous as the paranormal, it is very easy to rationalize and explain away failure.)

The burden for success, then, does not rest solely with the psychic. The investigator is an equally important part of the equation; if he or she does not create the proper conditions and have the proper attitude and expectation of success, this will likely be the direct cause of failure. This will not be attributed to himself or herself, of course, but will be mistakenly attributed to the psychic. The investigator can then self-righteously retreat, saying that he or she knew all along it was a bunch of hogwash.

Psychics repeatedly warn that there must be a genuine desire and need for the information requested. In other words, the motivation for obtaining information paranormally must be pure; the questioner's motives must not be for personal gain, recognition, power, money or any other selfish reason. A sincere investigator, then, working criminal cases for the benefit of the victim and society, seems to be in an ideal position for obtaining valid information paranormally.

An important consideration in dealing with psychics is communication, and to communicate well the investigator and psychic must understand each other. As mentioned previously, the investigator will become accustomed to the psychics' unusual vocabularies and worldviews. Because communication is a two-way street, the investigator must not assume that the psychics will understand the particular vocabulary, methods of investigation, criminal statutes, and elements needed to prove an offense. Most psychics will know little or nothing about this. Therefore, they will not know what type of information will be valuable to the investigation. As a result, it is an all-too-frequent experience for psychics to come up with valid but extraneous information, often to the exclusion of relevant information. For example, the aid of a psychic was enlisted by a sheriff's office to help locate the body of a boy presumed drowned in a river. Over the telephone the psychic said that all she could see was a snake, a motorcycle in the brush, and a man in a canoe. Another psychic told the investigating deputy to go up the river exactly six miles from town and he would find the body. He drove along the river for six miles and got out of his car. As he was walking down to the river bank, a snake crossed in front of him and he spotted a motorcycle hidden in the brush, which proved to be stolen. At the water's edge, he found the boy's body, at which point he looked up to see a man floating by in a canoe.

This case perfectly illustrates the necessity of a basic knowledge of investigation. The first psychic was able to provide valid but irrelevant information. The second psychic cut through the nonessentials and got to the heart of the matter. Conceivably, the first psychic may have done the same with a better understanding of what information was needed. (This case also illustrates the advantages of working with more than just one psychic. It often seems that each psychic has access to a piece of the puzzle but rarely has all the pieces.)

In another instance, the authors were testing a potential psychic by asking him to name the crime for which each of several individuals were convicted by looking at their mugshots. When looking at the picture of a bank robber, he said, "pilfering." We interpreted this as a miss, but later questioning revealed that he called robbery "pilfering." Similarly, other psychics confuse robbery with burglary.

For these reasons it is advisable for the investigator to educate the psychics in some basic vocabulary, elements needed to prove an offense, and investigative methods. This could be done immediately before each case is presented, by reading the statute, defining terms, and explaining what sort of information is needed to prove the offense. Such instruction will help each psychic focus their attention and efforts for more relevant information. The investigator is cautioned, however, that many times *seemingly irrelevant information later proves to be valuable.*

Just as the investigator and psychic must have a mutual understanding to work effectively and efficiently, the psychic must clearly understand the questions asked. For example, it seemingly would be a straightforward question to ask a psychic if a missing person is alive or dead. When the authors did this, however, we were continually frustrated by receiving contradictory replies from credible psychics. At the verge of giving the whole endeavor up, one particularly insightful psychic asked us if we had considered the possibility that the different psychic sources (i.e., the different levels of reality from which psychics gain their information) had differing definitions and perceptions of the states of being called "alive" and "dead." For instance, if life after death is a reality, then a person we would consider dead may appear quite alive to a psychic source. Yet another psychic source may define a planetside person who is a strict materialist and atheist as dead; such a person is "spiritually dead," which is more dead than being physically dead. Such explanations, no matter how seemingly implausible, must be considered and weighed carefully.

With this complication in mind, we began to formulate our questions more precisely, leaving no doubt as to what it was that we were asking. For example, instead of asking if a particular person is alive or dead, we would ask, "Is the person who goes by the name of John Doe planetside and currently alive in a physical body as we know it?" Although somewhat cumbersome, this form of precise questioning removed the problem of different perspectives, definitions, and perceptions and allowed for a greater degree of confidence in the psychics' answers. Such exacting questioning is not necessary with all psychics, however; it is an individual matter that can be clarified beforehand.

The investigator should be careful not to over-question. To do so will put undue pressure on the psychic and may encourage speculation. On the other hand, if a psychic provides contradictory or unclear information, the investigator should ask for clarification.

Although there are advantages to working with more than one psychic, as mentioned, this invites an inherent frustration; namely, what do you do with conflicting information? For instance, what do you do if you have five psychics and they disagree as to whether a missing man is alive or dead? First of all, the investigator should prioritize their responses on the basis of which psychics proved to be most accurate during the testing phase. (All psychics with whom an investigator is working should be periodically tested covertly by throwing in solved cases. They should also be checked for accuracy by withholding known information on unsolved cases currently being worked. In this way, the investigator can give relative weight to each response.) Secondly, ask each psychic to evaluate their own degree of confidence in their response and give priority to the most confident ones. (This should always be done as a matter of routine on all responses on all cases. Research has shown that gifted psychics can distinguish to a statistically significant degree between genuine psychic impressions and mere guesses. In this way the investigator can make a reasonable determination as to the merit of the conflicting responses.) Thirdly, simply tally the responses to determine whether there is a significant majority (e.g., alive versus dead).

To illustrate the degree of agreement that it is possible to achieve, the authors asked seventeen psychics if a murder victim knew her assailant; sixteen said yes, and one said no. The psychics were also asked if the murderer was a local resident or transient; sixteen said he was local, and one abstained. In another case a detective on a murder case theorized that the husband was guilty. Eleven psychics were asked if the husband was involved in any way. All eleven said no, and all derived their opinions independent of each other. Such an overwhelming response naturally forced the detective to reevaluate his position.

In working with a group of psychics, the investigator will usually get a great deal of information on each case and will have to sort out the leads to follow up on the basis of the degree of correlation between the different psychics' information, their degree of confidence, relevance, likely importance of each piece of information, and feasibility and cost-effectiveness in actually doing the follow-up investigation. Although there is often a considerable amount of correlation between different psychics' readings, they rarely will be the same. This is often due not to basic disagreements but is a matter of each psychic either seeing something that the others did not see or seeing it from a different perspective.

When psychic leads prove accurate and helpful to a case solution, there is a tendency to avoid giving the credit due the psychic and to usurp it for oneself and the department. It is not unusual to hear an investigator in this situation say, "Well, I actually suspected that," or "We'd have figured that out eventually anyway." One psychic sleuth wrote that "working with the police is a very thankless task." The psychic found that if he was successful, the police were "unwilling to admit that any psychic guidance is responsible." If he failed, they would ridicule or blame him. The authors' recommendation is to give credit when and where it is due, especially if you want to create and maintain a successful working relationship with psychics. Dr. Truzzi agrees: "There is . . . evidence that [the police] may want to avoid giving public credit to a psychic even when there are private admissions of the psychic's usefulness. Police who use psychics need to come out of the closet and provide scientific evaluators with the needed score sheets." The form and extent of credit given may be as little as acknowledgment on a personal, private basis (which will generally be the case with the investigator's pool of local psychics who work confidentially) to a press release (if a well-known psychic worked the case, in which event public credit is often the only payment they expect).

A similar and even more frequent tendency is for the department receiving psychically obtained information to not follow it up, at least with any serious effort. When the case is finally solved and some of the psychic information proves to be accurate, or even could have led directly to the case solution if actively pursued, the department may say that the psychic was of no help. In one such instance, a psychic provided information on a murder case that later proved to be accurate. When asked to comment on her participation, however, the sergeant in charge of the investigation, a diehard skeptic, replied, "To the best of my knowledge she hasn't helped us. We weren't pursuing her predictions." Perhaps the irony of this statement was lost to the sergeant; that is, the psychic was not of help to him, because he did not follow up her clues.

Any investigator using psychics, however, should be cautioned not to get locked into a psychic's theory of a crime before establishing his or her own theory on the basis of hard evidence. The investigator's own theory should be primary and should only be replaced by a psychic's theory on its merits and not because of its paranormal origin. Similarly, too much confidence should not be placed in any psychic, which may tempt the investigator to neglect other more traditional lines of inquiry. It must be remembered that all psychically produced information must be submitted to the rigors of traditional follow-up procedures. Homicide detective Keaton concurs: "Don't get tunnel vision. The investigator shouldn't get locked into the psychic's theory and try to prove it. It is mandatory that the investigator attempt to corroborate the psychic independently." Psychic investigator Jaegers agrees: "Don't *believe* anything. You need evidence."

The investigator needs to guard against the all too common tendency to believe psychically generated information just because it's psychically generated; that is, on the basis of its allegedly otherworldly source. This is particularly likely if the investigator has a strong belief in psychic abilities in general and in his or her psychics in particular. If this is the case, there is an inclination to rationalize or explain away failure, which is often all too easy to do given the frequently general or symbolic nature of the information provided. When it comes to evaluating psychic performance, which must be done on an ongoing basis, the investigator needs to be fair but as objective as possible. If it's working, the investigator (and department) needs to know; if it isn't working, they need to know that as well. The sympathetic investigator obviously wants the program to succeed, and to that end it is tempting to skew the results. On the other hand, the unsympathetic investigator will tend to do the opposite: interpret and skew the data toward failure, a tendency that needs to be guarded against as well. So, the investigator must avoid what is called a "false-positive" error of claiming something is there when in fact it is not, as well as the "false-negative" error of declaring something is not there when in fact it is. Both errors constitute bad procedure.

In evaluating one's psychics on actual casework, the investigator needs to insist on specific information; that is, a criterion for continuing to work with any psychic should be their ability to fairly consistently provide detailed and specific information. As psychic investigator Nancy Czetli says, "If you can't get precise detail, you're no use whatsoever to the police because they've got to have really concrete stuff." Dr. Broughton concurs: "There is much to suggest that the potential exists for a truly productive alliance, but this will require psychics to become more adept at recognizing the really important information."

Ironically, a potential problem—one that psychics are legitimately concerned about—is the possibility of being considered a suspect if they provide *too* detailed information, i.e., information that only the perpetrator could know. In a dramatic case in California, Etta Louise Smith, a mother of three and Lockheed Aircraft employee, told the police that she had a psychic vision of the murder of Melanie Uribe, a missing nurse. Because Ms. Smith's vision included facts about the killing known only to the police, she was booked for murder. She was held for four days, then released without charge. Ms. Smith sued the city of Los Angeles in 1987, and the jury awarded her damages for lost wages, attorney's fees, and pain and suffering. In a similar instance, a psychic associated with the Professional Psychics United Psychic Rescue Team was charged with murder after he walked into the Homewood, Illinois, Police Department and revealed details about a homicide. Unfortunately, it is this justifiable fear that keeps some otherwise good psychics from working with law enforcement.

The investigator developing a psychic investigation program must be very careful and discrete, lest the local press discover its use. Most media coverage is likely to do more harm than good, for several reasons. First, few reporters can handle the subject maturely, and it makes for sensationalistic stories. Second, media coverage will stimulate many would-be psychics to contact the department wanting to get involved in the project (among whom may be a few genuine ones, however). Third, the investigator in charge of the project will be continually hounded by the police reporters for progress reports and results. This could also lead to the identification of the participating psychics, breaching the promised confidentiality, hence compromising them personally and even professionally. Fourth, public criticism, especially from some local religious groups and "God squads," will be stimulated. The most familiar cry of alarm is that it's the devil's work. Such people are impossible to argue with because of their circular reasoning: If you support the use of psychics, which is the devil's work, then you are motivated by the devil. It should be perfectly understood, however, that as the mysteries of the paranormal are slowly giving way to science, it is becoming more apparent that psychic abilities and phenomena have little if anything to do with the esoteric and the occult. Most parapsychologists today are expressing the view that psychic abilities are innate in all people and are our natural birthright. From this perspective it is a very positive endeavor to attempt to explore and develop one's potential.

In conclusion, there are several factors influencing success in psychic investigation:

1. Finding the right psychics and determining how they work best, i.e., on what types of cases and with what techniques.
2. A mutual understanding of the project's purpose and objectives.
3. Educating the psychics on basic investigatory terminology, methods, and elements needed to prove the offense in question.
4. Psychic work needs to be low pressure, hence on their turf at a slow pace. If they request a certain set of working conditions, try to see that they are met (within reason).
5. Psychics work best when interested and motivated, hence the investigator should present interesting cases and motivate

them with feedback. Boredom and fatigue inhibit successful psychic work.

6. The investigator needs to be sympathetic and understanding, if not an outright believer. Parapsychological research has repeatedly shown that open skepticism and disbelief (a "show me if you can" attitude) serve as barriers to psychic communication and dilute psychics' abilities. A study conducted at the University of Edinburgh in Scotland revealed a positive correlation between the experimenter's belief in ESP and the ESP scores of subjects.

7. There must be a mutual respect and an amicable working relationship. The investigator should cultivate a team spirit and treat the psychic as a colleague. Dr. Charles Honorton, the former director of research in the Division of Parapsychology and Psychophysics at the Maimonides Medical Center's Department of Psychiatry in New York, found that whether or not experimenters smiled and greeted their subjects in a cold or friendly manner noticeably affected subject's ESP scores.

8. Do not have unrealistic expectations. The investigator has to accept a certain tolerance for error and ambiguity, because even the most gifted psychics make confident assertions that prove to be inaccurate. In addition, a psychic may provide accurate information on one case, but be totally inaccurate on another. Or he or she might get correct information on certain aspects of a case and incorrect information on others. Also, sometimes a psychic may get good impressions regarding a case but displace them to another case being worked.

9. Psychics should be used as an ongoing investigative aid and not merely as a last resort on major cases. Chief Kozenczak (ret.) agrees: "The use of psychics does not have to be limited to those incidents where there are few or no leads. Rather than as a last resort, psychics could be helpful on a more practical basis." If brought into cases early, they can provide information that will help steer the investigation, e.g., which suspects to concentrate on, location of possible evidence, or discerning MOs and motives. Furthermore, the quantity and quality of psychic impressions tends to be greater when the case is "hot."

A pilot study was conducted by the Los Angeles Police Department's Behavioral Science Services in 1979 to evaluate the use of psychics in the investigation of major crimes. After testing twelve psychics on two solved and two unsolved crimes, the researchers concluded that "the research data does not support the contention that psychics can provide significant additional information leading to the solution of major crimes." A follow-up study with twelve psychics, twelve homicide detectives, and eleven college students compared their responses from identical evidence from murder cases. The conclusion was that "the information that the psychics came up with was not any better than that of the two comparison groups." In fact, no one gave "any information that would have been useful investigatively." A study conducted at the Center for Investigative Psychology at The University of Liverpool in England arrived at a similar conclusion.

In light of the preeceding discussion on working with psychics, and without knowing the degree to which the LAPD and Liverpool researchers met the factors influencing success (no information of this nature is given in their report), the study results mean little. It certainly cannot be taken as a final statement on the use of psychics in investigations and may say more about how *not* to work with psychics. It may very well be that the studies' methodology (e.g., objective, impersonal, negative experimenter bias, on the experimenter's turf, designed for experimenter convenience and not the psychics, using untested psychics) precluded success and preordained failure. Dr. Wiseman, in his generally critical book, *Deception & Self-Deception: Investigating Psychics*, concludes that "it is difficult to know how conclusively these studies should be viewed, given that the methods and analyses used may have caused the researchers to have missed evidence of psychic functioning." Similarly, because of inherent methodological flaws, Swanson, Chamelin, and Territo in their text, *Criminal Investigation*, conclude that these studies do not provide "an answer to the general question of the usefulness of psychics in criminal investigation."

The degree to which psychics can be successful if used properly has been dramatically and convincingly demonstrated in archaeology. Archaeology is a unique testing ground for psychics, because it offers a hard scientific assessment of their accuracy, i.e., the psychic can be asked to locate an unknown archaeological site, describe the geology at different depths, and the type and age of artifacts to be found at what depths. The archaeologist then determines how accurate the psychic is through excavation. This presents an ideal testing situation, because it is triple-blind, i.e., not only do the psychic and archaeologist not know what is there beforehand, but nobody knows, hence ruling out the possibility of the psychic obtaining the information telepathically from some human source. In many instances, psychics have proved immeasurably valuable to archaeologists in their search for prehistoric sites and subsequent excavations and reconstructions of life as it was at that time. Innumerable man-hours spent on digging random test trenches and pits have been saved by psychically locating specific areas and depths.

A pioneering archaeologist-psychic team was composed of Dr. J. Norman Emerson, former president of the Canadian Archaeological Association, senior professor of anthropology at the University of Toronto, and revered "father of Canadian archaeology," and George McMullen, his psychic respondent. In many instances, McMullen accurately described and located long-buried artifacts and Indian structures, often giving depths accurate to within inches of their actual location. Subsequent excavation of several sites proved McMullen to be approximately 80 percent correct.

Another well-known and tested psychic, Aron Abrahamson, located an ancient man site in Flagstaff, Arizona, for the archaeologist Dr. Jeffrey Goodman. Before excavation began, Abrahamson made a series of thirty-four geological predictions (e.g., soil types, disconformities, and rock formations) and twenty-three archaeological predictions (e.g., type and ages of artifacts). Despite the scoffs of professional geologists and archaeologists, excavation proved Abrahamson's geological predictions 94 percent correct and his archaeological predictions 78 percent correct.

The research that has been done in psychic archaeology has some important ramifications for the use of psychics in criminal investigations. First, experience has clearly shown that success depends on the same variables identified in the authors' experience, namely: (1) properly identifying, recruiting, and thoroughly testing potential psychics; (2) developing a mutual language and understanding; (3) establishing a good working relationship based on mutual respect and trust; (4) having a positive researcher attitude and expectation of success; (5) having genuine and pure motives and goals; and (6) proper questioning and interpretation of the answers. Second, on many occasions the psychic readings on Indian sites seemed totally improbable and counter to all known archaeological evidence and theory, yet were proved to be true through subsequent excavation. The important lesson here is for the investigator not to dismiss outright a psychic reading from a previously accurate psychic just because it runs counter to his or her preconceptions of how the crime occurred. Follow-up investigation may in fact prove the psychic correct. Third, the psychic is not a panacea but must be combined with the best techniques that traditional investigation has to offer. The combination produces a synergistic effect, making it superior to either approach alone. Fourth, if a psychic is able to provide some verifiable information, the remainder of the information, even though presently unverifiable, should also be assumed to be reasonably accurate until proven otherwise.

In conclusion, the failure of the LAPD and Liverpool studies, may be ascribed to the failure of the researchers and their procedures, and not necessarily to the psychics per se.

Chapter 6

PSI CASE FILES

Psychic criminology is of little value if it does not produce positive results. The following actual cases demonstrate the usefulness of psi in investigations. Included are several cases in which psychically obtained information led directly to the case solution. Others are included–even though the information provided was not instrumental in solving the case–because they clearly demonstrate the type and quality of relevant information that is possible to obtain from psychics. Also, two brief accounts from declassified government remote viewing files will convey the investigative potential of RV in law enforcement.

MISSING MAN

"I am pretty confident that had I never gone to Mrs. Martin, Mr. Prado would still be up there, because we had searched the area several times," concluded Det. Sgt. Realyvasquez (personal communication). The Pacifica, California, resident Dennis Prado, a 71-year-old former United States Army paratrooper and Caltrans employee, was last seen on May 1, 1997. An extensive search, involving Pacifica Police Department and San Mateo County Sheriff Search and Rescue personnel, was conducted without success in the nearby 2,000-acre San Pedro Valley County Park where Prado liked to hike. At the request of Prado's sister, who also had been searching actively, Realyvasquez consulted with psychic Annette Martin on July 22, 1997, at her office in nearby Campbell, California, after obtaining permission from his superiors "because that's not something that we normally do."

Working with a photo of Prado and maps of the area, Martin said that she saw Prado leave his apartment and walk up a path through the woods. She saw him veer off the path toward a little hill where he sat to look at the vista, but then something happened. "I felt him clutch his left chest around his heart," she said. "He couldn't breathe and I felt him struggling to walk and falling on the ground amongst the underbrush. The sense that I had was that Mr. Prado had a heart attack, collapsed and died instantly. I didn't feel that there was any foul play. It was a natural death."

It was obvious to Realyvasquez that Martin was describing an area in the San Pedro Valley County Park, although Martin had never been there. Realyvasquez asked Martin if she could pinpoint the spot on the map of the park. Tracing the route that she felt Prado had taken, Martin finally drew a circle on the map around an area where she felt a "warm spot," indicative of where she said Prado fell and died. Although they had been searching the park for two months, Realyvasquez thanked Martin and said that he would organize a search of the area she indicated.

Realyvasquez shared Martin's information with search and rescue volunteer Roberta Hauser, who took it upon herself to search the area with a teammate and his specially trained German shepard, even though she had searched the area twice before. The searchers went to the area indicated and within twenty-five minutes found the body lying in the underbrush about fifteen feet off the trail. Because the body was in a fetal position, Realyvasquez said that "It looked like Mr. Prado may have gone and laid down," and every indication was that death was due to natural causes with no signs of foul play.

"If we didn't have that information, chances are he'd still be there because he was all dressed in green, covered up with brush, and embedded in the dirt." Realyvasquez noted. "Do I want to believe it? I don't have a choice. That's the honest answer."

Asked if Martin's information was instrumental in finding the body, Hauser (personal communication) replied "Absolutely! Annette described Mr. Prado's route and the area, and pinpointed the location of the body; it was right in the middle of the little eighth-mile diameter circle she'd drawn on the map. She also said that a person isn't going to find him, a dog is. This is the most amazing thing I've ever done. I was stunned!"

Asked if he would use Martin again, Realyvasquez said, "The only reason we did it is because the family requested it, and because of the relationship that was created between me and Mr. Prado's sister. Also, by that time a few months had passed. So basically, we did it as a favor to the family and as a last ditch effort. I got the approval to do it and we did it, but it's not normally our policy. But you can't knock it. It worked."

HOMICIDE

In autumn of 1975, Deputy Keith Wolverton of the Cascade County Sheriff's Department responded to a call of a possible homicide involving an elderly lady who was in her home near Great Falls, Montana. Wolverton (personal communication) tells the following story:

> When I arrived, I found her lying on the floor between her bedroom and dining room with multiple stab wounds. Officers were assigned to the case. Weeks later, after all leads failed and the investigation was nearing an end with no suspects, two officers, Undersheriff Glenn Osborne and myself, contacted a psychic. Neither of us had worked with one in the past, however we knew an officer in another county who had worked with a psychic named Harold Sherman. A call was made to Mr. Sherman in Little Rock, Arkansas. Getting to him was difficult. We had to explain in detail our case to the person who answered the telephone. We were told that if Mr. Sherman was able to take the case, he would call us back. A short time later, Mr. Sherman called back and we explained our case to him. Before replying, Mr. Sherman explained some of his other cases. I have always felt that he explained these cases to enable us to understand his sincerity in working with us. He impressed me as a gentleman with deep concern for our unsolved homicide. He was the first psychic that I ever (knowingly) talked with.

> I was amazed when he started to describe the house to us. Then he talked about a river [the Missouri River was nearby] and saw two young men, one throwing an object into the river from a bridge. He described both boys and indicated one had red hair. This conversation lasted about thirty minutes. We thanked him and continued our investigation. A short time later a Great Falls city police detective was told by an informant that a young man who lived across the river frequented the area where the homicide occurred. I contacted several businesses along the route and was told of a young boy who was always wandering around, didn't go to school, and lived in a trail-

er court. I went to the court and talked to the manager, describing the boy. He said he knew the boy and pointed out the trailer.

After knocking on the door several times an elderly woman opened the door about one inch. I identified myself and she opened the door a little further. I told her I was looking for a boy who might live here. She replied, "He doesn't live here," and started to close the door when I observed a boy about sixteen standing behind her. He had red hair! I looked directly at him and told him I wanted to talk to him. He said, "Sure, what about?" I placed him in the patrol car and talked to him. After a short time I felt it imperative to take him in for further questioning. Before the day ended, he was arrested for the homicide.

Later, I received a call from the Bakersfield, California, Sheriff's Department. They had a young man in their jurisdiction who admitted killing the woman.

Detective Dick Duncan and I went to Bakersfield and obtained a statement from the second boy. He stated he was alone when he killed the woman. He described how he disposed of the knife by thrusting it into a wooden post connecting a guard rail to the bridge, then breaking off the handle and throwing it into the river. A phone call was made to Undersheriff Osborne. With that information, he was able to retrieve the knife from the post.

It was later determined that the red-headed boy was only a witness and was afraid to tell what he had seen. He subsequently was released and a conviction was obtained on the second boy.

Wolverton commented that he will "never forget how Mr. Sherman was able, over the phone, to give us detailed data regarding an area he had never seen and about a violent crime he knew nothing about until minutes before."

MISSING WOMAN

Beverly Jaegers of the U.S. PSI Squad was consulted by the authors about a missing person, Hope Sage, a retired nurse in Missoula County, Montana. Sage had been missing for several years, and the case was considered at a dead end. Working with only the missing woman's name, Jaegers said that Sage had gone up a small mountain near her home, where she died. There was no indication of murder, she said, rather the woman died of a stroke. Acting on this information, one of the authors searched and found a human skull up a mountain behind the woman's home. Subsequent analysis by the Smithsonian Institution determined that the skull was that of a female approximately the same age as the missing woman. The woman had left a suicide note in her home. The cause of death remains unknown, and there was no evidence of foul play. As a result, the case was closed.

DOUBLE HOMICIDE

On October 17, 1987, Candace Augustus and her 11-year-old son, Gregory, were found bludgeoned to death with a baseball bat in their mobile home in the Village of Dixmoor, Illinois, a south Chicago suburb. According to then-Chief Anton Graff (personal communication), during the crime scene investigation Illinois State Police Evidence Technician Dexter Bartlett suggested psychic Bill Ward as a possible resource to use in the investigation. Although suspect about using a nontraditional method at such an early stage of the investigation, Graff consented because "there were numerous unknown factors of why such a brutal murder occurred [and] we needed assistance profiling the crime scene and possible offender. Bill Ward was a source we thought could provide some insight." That is exactly what happened.

At the time of the first contact with Ward, the investigators had reason to believe that the crime might be racially or drug related, that Gregory was killed because he witnessed his mother's murder, and that a possible suspect, the now-absent, live-in boyfriend, Robert Fair, was headed to California as claimed by Candace's friends. This stood to reason, because Fair had lived in California before the murder, plus he had family and a live-in girlfriend there. Furthermore, given the heinous nature of the crime, the investigators believed that Fair would not return home to his mother in Mississippi, because she knew and loved Gregory. In addition, investigators called the local sheriff in Mississippi, who said that Fair was not there so there was no need to go there.

Ward believed otherwise. In a conference call with Graff and Sgt. Schwartzkopf, Ward focused on Fair and insisted that he had gone home to his mother in Mississippi. He also claimed that Fair did not take his vehicle to Mississippi but had ditched it approximately one-and-a-half to two hours from Dixmoor. Ward further insisted that if the family (other than the mother) knew the truth and was shown the crime scene pictures, they would be so upset that they would probably turn Robert in. "Don't be afraid of showing the picture, but try to stay away from Mom, try to find another family member," he said.

Ward also provided a lot of other information, including confirmed but unpublicized details of the crime. As a result, Graff decided to follow his advice: "Since Ward was right on a lot of other things as judged by the evidence that came back from the coroner and evidence tech about how the people were killed, maybe we should take Bill's advice. It's not going to hurt and will only be a day delay on the way to California." So Graff instructed his investigators, Schwartzkopf and Morgan, to go to Mississippi.

On the way to Mississippi on I-57 they passed Bloomington, Illinois. Shortly after, Graff received a call from the Bloomington police who found Fair's car at the local bus station. "That really sparked up Sgt. Schwartzkopf and made all of us all more believers in what Ward was telling us because when you look at the map it's an hour-and-a-half to two hours away and along the main expressway to Mississippi."

Once in Mississippi, Schwartzkopf and Morgan interviewed Fair's mother and brother, and on Ward's advice, showed the picture of Gregory to the brother. The brother admitted that Robert had been there but had left. Schwartzkopf called Graff that night saying that they were going to leave for California. Graff instructed them to sit tight until he could call Ward. Later that night Graff called Ward who insisted, "Tell them not to leave. He's there. I don't see him traveling from there. Tell your guys to wait a day." Graff called Schwartzkopf and Morgan at the hotel and instructed them not to leave. "I don't want you guys to leave, Bill thinks he's there." Graff admitted that he could hear the skepticism in their voices, so he said, "Hey guys, he hasn't been wrong yet. Come on, it's not going to hurt the investigation. For another day you guys nose around down there." The next morning Graff's phone rang, and Schwartzkopf told him that he had just received a call from the county sheriff's office saying that Robert Fair is in their station. His brother brought him in, and Robert turned himself in.

Schwartzkopf and Morgan went right over to the sheriff's office.

Asked why Robert turned himself in, the brother confided that "When you guys showed me the picture, and when you were at my Mom's place Robert was out in the field hiding. The other reason I convinced him to turn himself in is that he killed one of his own kind." So Fair turned himself in and voluntarily submitted to a formal interview.

Recollecting the original conference call with Ward, Schwartzkopff remembered that Ward said Fair would be ready to break when he started bringing his head and shoulders down and putting his thumbs into his hands. "At that moment show him the picture of Gregory. He'll confess," Ward had instructed. During the interview Schwartzkopf noted that Fair's posture was getting weaker and finally when his thumbs curled in he opened his folder and said, "Look at this." Seeing Gregory's picture, Fair broke down crying and confessed.

According to Schwartzkopf, Ward provided important insight into the offender's mind, which facilitated the interrogation. Specifically, Ward pinpointed the motive when he said that Robert believed that he had to kill Gregory, because there'd be nobody left to take care of him once he went to jail for killing his mom. Armed with this information, Schwartzkopf (personal communication) said that he

> felt more confident during the interview, like I already knew him and the reason he killed Gregory. This "inside information" enhanced my ability to obtain a confession by providing for a more relaxed atmosphere during the interview, which is a key element for a successful interview as stated in my training with the Reid Interview and Interrogation class. I felt I had an edge and less pressure to obtain the confession.

Schwartzkopf stated that if one could compare the interview with Robert Fair with Ward's reading "you would see why I encourage exploring the option for the use of a psychic in criminal investigations." For instance, Ward said that Fair struck Gregory in the head with the bat four, possibly five times, each strike less forceful than the one before. Fair voluntarily confessed this during the interview. Furthermore, the evidence technician's blood splatter analysis determined four or five blows.

Graff said, "The confession in all its detail was probably 98 to 99 percent what Bill said the guy did, even down to the point that Bill said the Dixmoor police came close to catching him the first night. 'He was at a local gas station,' Ward had told us, 'and one of your officers was there. Robert wanted to walk up to that officer and tell him about the crime, but he wanted to go home and say something to his Mom.'" In his confession Fair admitted that when he left the crime scene, he went to a gas station and there was an officer whom he wanted to tell. "It just blew Schwartzkopf's mind," notes Graff. "It was as if in some way or form Ward was in Robert's mind and knew what he was thinking and doing."

Graff said Ward's character profile and advice during the interrogation process coincided with what the investigators obtained through more traditional methods. Without Ward's help, he said, solving this case would have taken more time. "It was a very rewarding learning experience for myself and other officers that were involved," Graff noted. "I think that law enforcement should know that these types of individuals are out there and have been tested in the field. From a cop to other cops, I think that those who have an inkling to try something new should use people like Bill as another resource."

When asked whether Ward's information was helpful in apprehending Robert Fair and in solving the crime, Graff replied "Yes it was. Besides providing detailed information about the crime and character profile and whereabouts of the offender, Bill was instrumental as a coach, as a provider of that energy level that's necessary to keep an investigation going. You know, in an investigation you sometimes hit that wall, and you wonder what the next step is. But Bill was like a cheerleader, I mean he would just pick us up or allow that brainstorming, that creativity that you need in an investigation, to give us a little push, and not to focus in just one area."

Robert Fair confessed to both murders and is currently sitting on death row in Illinois.

MISSING PERSON

Locked in a bitter child custody battle, a young woman from Kodiak, Alaska, agreed to meet with a man who said he had information that her ex-husband planned to use against her. As reported by Gayle Pasternak in *Tour of Duty: The Diaries of Psychic Bill Ward*, a private investigator was hired by the woman's lawyer to follow her to the meeting place. When the woman got into the man's white van, the PI drove around a building to establish a better observation point. In the short time he did not have the vehicle in view it disappeared, and the woman with it.

The van was recovered, but the woman was never seen again.

Three arrests were made and murder charges filed. The trial result-ed in the acquittal of one defendant and hung juries on the remaining two. A second trial was set in Anchorage to ensure an impartial jury. About one week before trial, Detective Mike Andrey was browsing through the current issue of *Law and Order* magazine, which featured Bill Ward. He called Mr. Ward. Andrey explained that his case was built on circumstantial evidence and that he needed something solid to tie the victim to the suspect's van.

"There's a piece of jewelry in that van," Ward told him, "about eighteen to twenty-four inches from the driver's seat."

A pierced earring clasp had been found between the seats by the Alaska State Crime Lab, but their thorough search of the vehicle revealed no earring.

"Look again," Ward told Andrey. "It's there."

Andrey and Sergeant John Palmer returned to the impound lot. Andrey crawled into the back of the van while Palmer stood outside the passenger side examining the front console with a flashlight. Suddenly, a tiny glint of light caught his eye.

"Mike, Mike! Get out here and look!"

As Andrey joined him on the passenger side, Palmer instructed him to follow the beam of light as he aimed below the dash. An auxiliary oil pressure gauge had been installed and there, propped between two tiny wires, was a delicate ivory earring, later identified by the missing woman's aunt as one she had gifted to her niece.

The new evidence was too good to be true according to the defense attorneys, who attempted to shroud its validity with the suspicion that the earring had been planted.

On November 22, Andrey was called to the stand. The defense's line of questioning was intended to make him appear foolish for hav-ing appealed to a psychic thousands of miles away and, further, for expecting a jury to believe that the psychic really helped.

But questions from the prosecution actually reinforced the credibil-ity of their find:

> "So, the psychic told you to look in the van for a piece of jewelry eighteen to twenty-four inches from the driver's seat. Is that correct?" the defense attorney asked.

"Yes," Andrey confirmed.

"Did you find it?"

"Yes."

"Can you describe that piece of jewelry?"

"It was a small, ivory, pierced earring with a blue hand-painted flower on it."

"Did the earring belong to the victim?"

"Yes."

"No further questions."

The ex-husband and the man he hired to murder his wife were found guilty.

MURDERED GIRL

Gloria de la Cruz kissed her seventeen-year-old daughter goodnight on April 23, 1996, and went to bed. The next morning her daughter, Babash, was gone. A frantic search was begun in that coastal city of Oxnard, California. Seventeen days later, the police called to inform de la Cruz that her daughter had been found murdered and dumped in a trash bin sixty miles away in Los Angeles. De la Cruz asked Pam Coronado, a psychic and licensed private investigator, for help after rumors had spread of her success finding the body of a local missing woman.

In her reading, Coronado said that Babash had been raped and murdered by a local man who had driven her to a remote area along the Pacific Coast Highway. After strangling her he continued on the highway to dump her in Los Angeles. Coronado stated that Babash knew the man and that she had gone with him willingly. She further stated that he was in his early twenties, drove a green mid-sized car, lived in Oxnard, and that his name was similar to "Rosengren."

De la Cruz relates what happened next (personal communication):

When Babash first went missing we were frantic. We went to every one of her friends that we could think of. We asked for help or any information we could get to help find her. She was a popular mariachi singer and often performed at parties. I had spoken to everyone I could think of except one. She had a male friend who was in jail. So my other daughter Corinna and I went to the jail to speak to him.

We stepped into the elevator to go to the third floor. The elevator stopped on the second floor and two men got in. They were going down and we were going up. One of the men looked at my daughter Corinna and said, "Don't I know you?" She replied that she did not think so. The man insisted that she looked familiar.

It struck me that it was Babash that he knew. His name was Robinson and I had met him once when he came to the house to see Babash. He was not the man we had gone to the jail to see. I told him that Babash was missing and asked if he could help us. He didn't seem too concerned and I thought that was odd. But I gave him my number and asked him to call me. He never did.

This raised de la Cruz's suspicions. Furthermore, struck by the similarity with the information provided by Coronado (i.e., a young man known to Babash with a name similar to Rosengren, who lived in Oxnard and drove a green mid-sized car, all true) as well as the coincidental meeting in the elevator, de la Cruz gave Robinson's name to the case detective.

Robinson was later arrested, charged with murder, and sentenced to life in prison without the possibility of parole.

De la Cruz says, "If Robinson had not stepped into that elevator at that exact moment, I never would have thought of him and given his name to police. We could have missed him by just seconds. It was a miracle." (More likely this was a prime example of a *synchronicity* discussed at length in Chapter 7.)

MULTIPLE CHILD ABDUCTION

The author asked a psychic investigator for help on a multiple child abduction case.[1] She said that I should go to a certain ranch house way

---

[1] Because this case involves minors there is a need for confidentiality. Therefore locations and names have been excluded.

out in the desert where I would find a person who would know where the abducted children were. On the basis of this information, I asked the local law enforcement agency to surveil the house to determine when the individual who lived there was available to be talked to. The psychic was getting strong impressions that this person was the key to finding these children and should be approached. Eventually spotting a woman there, I suggested that we call her and see if we could set up an informal meeting. When the woman answered the phone, we identified ourselves and said that we were calling to see if she had seen the children or the abductors. She indicated that she had no knowledge of them and to leave her alone. (We learned later that she was a sister of one of the abductors.)

The psychic kept saying that if we could not get the cooperation of the woman, we needed to get into the house, because we would find information that would lead us to the children. Assuming that the psychic was right and that the woman was covering up for the perpetrators who had abducted the children, we were ready to obtain a search warrant.

At this point a federal law enforcement agency contacted us and advised strongly to "stand down," not to bother this woman anymore, and that they were taking over the case. Not very happy with the federal intervention in their case, the local law enforcement agency decided not to stand down. They were eventually able to gain information from the woman that took them right to the children. Arrests were made, and the children were returned safe and unharmed.

Information obtained directly from the psychic informant was instrumental in solving this case. Without the psychic's help, this case might not have had a happy ending.

MURDERED WIFE

In the spring of 1986 Detective Bob Lee of the Lake Oswego Police Department in Oregon had "a missing persons case that became a homicide real quick," as he commented. Alexis Sara Burke had disappeared after having an argument with her husband John. Lee interviewed friends and relatives and conducted an exhaustive search, but had few solid clues and lots of questions. Lee tells the following story (personal communication):

We had some inquiries in the past from other police agencies about Laurie McQuary. She was a psychic who was known to work with cops once in a while. She lived and worked here in town, but my department didn't know anything about her; we'd never had any contact with her. And I sure had not, because it is not my style or my personality to be involved with psychics.

So now I wanted to contact Laurie myself for several reasons, the biggest of which to find out exactly what she knew about my missing person. When I phoned Laurie about setting up a meeting, she almost didn't agree. I went to her office, and at first I thought I'd gone to the wrong place. It was a business office that looked like an attorney's or accountant's office, with no plywood sign, no palm print. And I was looking at a very attractive, dark-haired lady wearing a dressy, feminine business suit instead of purple robes. Somehow, I felt a little better.

Laurie told me 30 things about my case: who, what, when, where, how come, who knew about it, a description of the car used to transport the body, and stuff like that. I was intrigued. Some of what she was saying I did indeed know to be true, and some other things I was almost 100 percent certain about. Laurie said that John had killed his wife, that he strangled her. She also said a whole circle of people around John and his younger brother, Scott, knew all about it.

Laurie went on to describe the victim's car, the area where it would be found, and a slew of other things, I tried to take her comments as seriously as I could, but I had one problem: a lot of what she said had to do with Scott. A student at a local college, he had been in California playing baseball for the school team during the time frame in question. We had proved that beyond a doubt. So he was pretty much out of the equation, yet Laurie insisted that Scott had helped John bury his wife. Then she told me where to find the body. "It's 15 miles southwest of here, near water," she said. I raised one eyebrow. "This is Oregon, gimme a break! Everything is near water!"

Okay, so that was flip. So I suggested that we'd check a few places "near water," which we did, as well as try to find a place Laurie had mentioned called Bell's Landing. She said it was significant to the victim. We pored over geological survey maps but found nothing. So I decided she was wrong about that one. After spending four or five days running down some of Laurie's leads and chatting with people she named, we still didn't have anything close to a prosecutable case. We didn't have a body. I was irritated. Laurie worked with me for about a month, then she was off the case, and I was left with her information.

> John Burke worked at his dad's metal fabrication plant. John swore he had
> no idea where his wife had gone. Everything we knew about John's person-
> ality said that if we pressured him enough, he'd tell a lot of people what
> he'd done. John ended up telling everyone what he had done; unfortunate-
> ly no one was telling me!

Approximately a year-and-a-half later, a former girlfriend of John's
surfaced and told Lee several things that helped the investigation,
including the curious fact that John became anxious every time they
drove past a large field next to the plant where he worked. Even
though he never told her where he had buried his wife's body, the
girlfriend had a hunch he'd buried her in that field. She also knew that
John's best friend was his brother, Scott, and that if John had confided
in anyone it would have been his brother. She knew Scott well enough
to know that his roommate probably knew about it, as well as Scott's
two former roommates. Follow-up questioning of the roommates
revealed that, just as McQuary said, a circle of people around John
and Scott knew all about the murder, and that Scott had helped John
bury the body. So, in fact, Scott was involved heavily in the case as
intuited by McQuary.

The truth was that John had killed his wife and Scott had helped
bury her, but how could Scott have done that when he was out of
town at the time? Lee explains:

> You know, just when you think you've heard and seen it all, you hear one
> better. As it turned out, John was so helpless without Scott around that he
> couldn't even get it together to dispose of Alexis's body by himself. So he
> stashed her behind the living room sofa until Scott got back to town 36
> hours later. . . . We picked up Scott, he copped to everything, and agreed to
> take us to Alexis' body . . . buried in the field next to the metal fabrication
> plant. When the forensic team found her skull only five minutes into the
> digging, I was suddenly awed by the fact that the grave was less than a mile
> from where Laurie had said to look for it, and it was indeed near water—a
> little creek that literally touched the edge of the gravesite.

John Burke was arrested, charged with murder, and received a twen-
ty-year sentence on a plea arrangement.

"As it turned out," said Det. Lee, "28 of the 30 things Laurie had said
during our initial conversation were absolutely right on the money. . . .
As for the 29th thing, it was true, too. A couple years ago, John decided
he wanted to get things off his chest and make apologies to the people

he'd lied to. So I went to the penitentiary to chat with him. John said that when he and Alexis used to go hiking around McMinnville, Oregon, they would spend time at a place known locally as Bell's Landing! It actually had significance for both of them. And the 30th thing? Somehow I can't even remember what that was now."

"So that's how it went," concludes Det. Lee. "The case was solved and I'd had a psychic experience. We originally shot down a lot of what Laurie said because it had so much to do with Scott, and we simply did not think he could have been involved." Lee admits that even with the intuitive insights from McQuary "the case was solved by normal investigative procedures, but Laurie was terrifically accurate with everything we documented on June 3, 1986."

MURDERED PRIEST

On a warm Saturday night on August 4, 1982, Santa Fe, New Mexico police officer Dennis Miller (personal communication) remembers receiving a "10-65" (prepare to copy) "BOLO" (be on the lookout) dispatch for Father Reynaldo Rivera, a Franciscan Priest from St. Francis Cathedral. Father Rivera had received a telephone call at the rectory from a male caller at 8:35 P.M. who requested the priest meet him at the Interstate 25 rest area located about 13 miles south of Santa Fe to administer the last rights to his dying sister. The caller stated that he would be waiting by a telephone booth at this location. As a member of the Special Unit Division with a 95 percent completion record, Miller was assigned by the Chief of Police to the case.

On August 7 at 10:30 A.M., Father Rivera's body was found in an open field just off the dirt road leading to Waldo, New Mexico, two miles south of the rest area where he was supposed to meet the caller. Miller examined the body at the scene:

Father Rivera's body was resting on its back. His arms were extended out to either side and his legs were slightly apart. He had on a black shirt, black trousers secured with a black leather belt and black shoes. His eyes were opened as though he had seen the Devil himself. His eyes appeared to be greenish/grey with tear stains running from both corners. The three-strand barbed wire used to strangle him was still wrapped around his mouth and head several times and so tight that it was embedded into his facial skin. His chest and the black shirt had the imprint of a right shoe print as though he had been stomped. His shirt was partially open to reveal the chest area where slice marks from a sharp object had been made in an "X" and criss-crossed pattern.

Unfortunately, heavy rains during the previous two nights had destroyed much physical evidence, and other investigative efforts turned up no promising leads. Frustrated, Miller reviewed the case with fellow detectives at the Santa Fe Police Department. Detective Dan Chappell suggested that Miller request the assistance of a psychic from California, Annette Martin, with whom he had worked on a case—with impressive results. "As Detective Chappell spoke I became more interested," Miller said. "I was always willing to try something new. Chappell spoke very highly of Annette so I decided right then and there to seek her assistance. Her powers to feel and see the unknown were phenomenal according to Detective Chappell."

Miller wrote to Martin. He introduced himself, said that he was investigating a high-profile case and requested her assistance. He included a small black-and-white photo of Father Rivera with his name, date of birth, and the date of disappearance, and nothing else.

Several weeks later Miller received a package from Martin with a cassette tape, sketches, a letter, and the small photograph of Father Rivera. Miller was unprepared for what he was about to hear and read. "Everything that Ms. Martin described and sketched was consistent with what we knew about the case, *everything*. She was so precise. She described in horrifying detail how she believed Father Rivera died a death that is not imaginable." As Miller recounts it:

> In listening to the tape it was apparent that Ms. Martin placed herself into a state to where she was seeing and speaking of the actions that led to the death of the priest. As this was taking place, Ms. Martin was drawing and sketching on a piece of paper as to what she was seeing. Remember, the only information sent to Ms. Martin was a photo of the priest, date of birth, and the date of disappearance. Ms. Martin said that Father Rivera had been called out under false pretenses. He was lured to a place where cars could be seen parked with tables. Two side-by-side telephone booths could also be seen. The person who had requested the priest met him near the telephone booths. This all describes the rest area south of Santa Fe on I-25 where the male caller requested the priest meet him. Father Rivera was then instructed to follow the man. Ms. Martin could see a green sign with some writing on it, including the letter "W" along with a small letter "a" and small letter "l." By this sign she saw a bridge and dirt. This describes the green highway

sign for the Waldo Exit a couple of miles south of the rest area off I-25. The roadway leading to Waldo turns to dirt. Ms. Martin said that Father Rivera was led to a small shack or dwelling of sorts a few miles from this sign. When the priest entered, he looked around and saw nothing and inquired as to what was happening. Martin said that he was immediately jumped and assaulted, being bound with his hands behind his back with barbed wire. While he was pleading to know what was happening, Father Rivera was made to drop to his knees where someone who was behind him bound his face around the mouth with barbed wire and did so that it embedded into his facial skin.

While this was going on, Martin described another male subject standing in front of the priest demanding that he, Father Rivera, plead for his life. While the priest was being gagged, this subject slashed the chest of the priest with a long-blade knife. While the victim was screaming and trying to question why, the slashing continued in an "X" pattern. The subject standing behind the priest cannot be made out in physical description, but the other can. Martin described this man as a possible Mexican national, deformed in a way that he walks with a limp and is slightly twisted as he stands and walks. His hair is dark in color, possibly dark brown, and curly, not quite collar length. His hands are rough and calloused as those of a working man and he has great strength in them. Additionally, Martin described a beat-up blue Ford long-bed pickup which she says belonged to the suspect, and she saw a business establishment called The Pink Poodle. Our primary suspect matched this description, drove a pickup as described by Martin, and had worked at a motel/restaurant in Santa Fe called The Pink Abode.

Ms. Martin goes on to say that the holy articles used to administer the last rites to a dying person are placed next to the priest. She is breathing hard, as though she is gasping for air. Her voice reveals a horror that words cannot describe. She can feel the pain, suffering, and the infliction of the knife blade against his chest. Father Rivera is kicked in the chest by the subject standing in front of him causing him to fall backwards. The sight that Father Rivera has in front of him is so horrifying that he dies with his eyes open. slightly squinched as if he had seen Hell. The priest is taken to a location with no trees surrounding the area. His body is placed on the ground and left alone.

For unknown reasons Miller was reassigned and instructed to turn over the case to the New Mexico State Police. Although this case has never been solved, Miller was singularly impressed with the information provided by Martin: "Ms. Martin was never given any details of the case nor the condition of the body as it was found or even where it was discovered. Yet, her verbal statement, sketches and description of the area and location by name, condition of the body and items believed to have been used in the murder, the description of the suspect and his vehicle, all are as accurate as can be, all the way to the last details."

KIDNAPPING

In 1981 General James Dozier, senior officer in charge of NATO's Southern European command, was kidnapped by the Red Brigade in Italy. Remote viewers at Ft. Meade, the United States government's RV training center, were ordered to seek psychic clues about Dozier's whereabouts. The viewers said that he was being held in Pádova and was near a supermarket in a blue tent. This information was discounted at the time by the RV team supervisor Dale Graff, a physicist who was once in charge of advanced technology for the United States Air Force. As the liaison between the viewers and United States intelligence agencies, Graff decided not to pass the information on. Because Dozier was kidnapped in Verona and not Pádova, and because the information about the supermarket and blue tent made little sense, Graff reasoned that the viewers must be mistaken.

Several weeks later Dozier was rescued by the SAS in Pádova, where he was being held in a blue tent in an apartment above a supermarket.

FUGITIVE

Charles Jordon, a top United States customs agent had succumbed to bribes and used inside information to facilitate the smuggling of drugs into Florida. He was arrested but escaped, becoming America's most wanted fugitive. Although the authorities suspected that Jordon was in the Caribbean region, a government remote viewer said that Jordon was camping and on the move in Wyoming. William Greene, an official on the case, alerted the Wyoming authorities. Jordon was arrested soon after leaving a national park in his recreational vehicle near the area the remote viewer indicated.

Chapter 7

PSI ON THE JOB

The primary purpose of this book is to educate the interested investigator in how to use psychics as an investigative aid. A few references, however, have been made to the role of gut feelings, hunches, intuition, and even precognitive dreams in the peace officer's personal experience. Although it is not a purpose of this book to serve as a training manual for developing one's own latent psychic capability, the role of psi on the job nevertheless should be recognized, because it is potentially valuable to the investigator. In fact, a few law enforcement agencies have sponsored seminars and in-service training on the use of psi. The main idea was to develop the psi abilities of their own officers, which would hopefully accomplish two objectives: (1) to help the officers in their investigative work, thereby increasing clearance rates; and (2) dispensing with the need to use psychics outside the department, thereby avoiding all the attendant problems and pitfalls. One such agency was the Pomona Police Department, which wanted to train its detectives to use their intuition and imagination in case work. The authors highly recommend that law enforcement and criminal justice agencies pursue this type of training. In the absence of department-sponsored training, however, any interested officer can pursue training on his or her own, either through a local course on intuition or psi development or through the guidance of a book on the subject, such as *The Mind Race: Understanding and Using Psychic Abilities* by Russell Targ and Keith Harary, both reputable psi researchers, or *The Psychic Paradigm: A Psychic Reveals the Secrets of Unlocking Your Own ESP Abilities*, by Beverly Jaegers, a veteran psychic investigator. We believe that there is nothing to lose and everything to gain by peace officers learning to develop their own psi capability, whether telepathy, clairvoyance, precognition, dowsing, psychometry, remote viewing, or simply intuition.

The role of psi in investigation should not be diminished. It can be of tremendous help to the investigator, who should not discredit flashes of insight, intuitive revelations, or significant dreams. The history of science and business is replete with stories of famous scientists and businesspersons solving complex problems and answering difficult questions through these same nonanalytical means. For example, René Descartes, the founder of modern science, had a visionary experience that revealed to him "the foundations of a marvelous science"; Albert Einstein attributed his theory of relativity to a flash of insight; Kekulé, the famous German chemist, while dozing in front of his fireplace, dreamed the benzene molecule, a discovery heralded as "the most brilliant piece of prediction to be found in the whole of organic chemistry"; Michael Faraday intuited the notions of magnetic and electric fields; Alexander Poniatoff, founder of Ampex Corporation, admitted the important role of intuition in his business decisions; and William Keeler, former board chairman of Phillips Petroleum, stated that "oil fields have been found on hunches [and] through precognitive dreams." The famous scientist, architect, and writer, Buckminster Fuller, examined the diaries of great scientists and inventors to find a common denominator: "The most important item in connection with their great discovery . . . was intuition." The philosopher Bertrand Russell maintained that scientists need both intuition and logic, the first for generating ideas and the second for evaluating their truth. Similarly, investigators may intuit solutions to major cases, then follow up with logic. This represents an optimal "whole-brain" way of approaching investigation; that is, balancing "left brain" functions (logical, linear, rational, verbal) with "right brain" functions (intuitive, artistic, pattern recognition, wholistic). The synergistic effect of the two working together is superior to either working singly.

Another major aspect of psi on the job is its survival value. Dennis Nagy, former chief of police in Carteret, New Jersey, has taugcht RV courses to police officers. His training stressed officer survival and focused primarily on the street officer, not detectives: "It's probably more valuable to the street cop to increase their intuition. It's pure survival. If you figure out how many cops are killed in the line of duty, you'd be hard pressed to say that five were killed during an investigation, but of the two to three hundred cops who are killed each year across this country, many are killed with their own weapons because their guard was down. So I stress that if their intution was up, they might have exercised more care. It'd give them an edge." Similarly, Sgt. Keaton counsels "police recruits to cultivate their sixth sense, instincts, gut feelings, the thing inside that tells you 'Don't go there.' These are the same abilities that psychics have, only they've refined them."

Dr. Rex Stanford, director of the Center for Parapsychological Research in Texas, has developed a concept called *PSI-Mediated Instrumental Response* (PMIR) to explain nonintentional psychic experiences, usually nonconscious in nature. His research has demonstrated that each person constantly uses psi in addition to the five physical senses to scan the environment for information that will serve the needs of the individual. This scanning seems to be automatically carried out without conscious intention or awareness. It is hypothesized, then, that this "psychic radar" works continually on nonconscious levels, and when it detects something in the environment of survival value to the individual it automatically triggers the necessary behavioral response. On a conscious level the individual may not be able to rationally explain the reasons for the behavior and will ascribe it to something else, like coincidence or a hunch. For instance, a retired army colonel from New York "absentmindedly" got off the subway at the wrong exit only to bump into the people he was going to visit.

Some research studies demonstrate the probable existence of PMIR. One of the most convincing statistical studies involved the accumulation and analysis of passenger data for twenty-eight trains involved in accidents. It was found that there were significantly fewer passengers on the same trains beginning one week before the accident. There were also fewer people on the derailed and damaged cars compared with what was normal for nonaccident days. In some manner, and at some level of awareness, some people apparently knew or felt that the trains were not safe on those particular days and hence avoided them.

Another dramatic example of the survival value of PMIR occurred in Beatrice, Nebraska. The fifteen members of the local church choir met faithfully every night at 7:20 sharp for practice. On the evening of March 31, 1950, no one showed up (a chance probability of a billion to one)! At 7:25 the church boiler blew up and demolished the church, but no one was hurt, because no one was there. When asked afterwards, each choir member had some improbable reason for not being there. The obvious conclusion is that the choir members unconsciously intuited the future, gained information that had survival value, and fortunately acted on it.

Similarly, there are reported cases of people not boarding an airplane because of strong PMIR responses. In one example, author Elizabeth Kubler-Ross, M.D., was scheduled to leave her home in Chicago for a lecture in Florida. At O'Hare Airport she literally heard a voice tell her not to go. With the knowledge that an auditorium full of people would be waiting for her appearance, she reluctantly boarded the plane, only to hear the voice again. At the last minute, she got up and deboarded. The jetliner went down in the Everglades killing all aboard.

In controlled laboratory experiments at the University of Illinois, Dr. Norman Don demonstrated that the human brain does in fact respond unconsciously to future events. He concluded that "psi information does get into the brain," although the exact mechanism is unknown.

Studies on the physiological sensitivity of humans has also supported the existence of PMIR. Experimental subjects were hooked up to a plethysmograph (a device for measuring blood volume), an electroencephalograph, and a device for measuring galvanic skin response. The subjects were asked to guess when a "subliminal stimulus" was being directed to them. Unbeknownst to the subjects, a person in another room was periodically being administered a mild electric shock. The subjects' guesses did not correlate with the shocks, yet their physiological measurements showed abrupt changes whenever the shocks were administered.

A more dramatic demonstration of this nonconscious connection between living organisms comes from an experiment with animals. Russian scientists implanted electrodes deep in the brain of a mother rabbit, then killed her newborn babies at intervals at sea in a submarine. The mother, who was in a laboratory on the mainland, showed sharp electrical responses in her brain waves at the precise moment that each was killed.

The implication of these research findings is that living organisms are indeed much more sensitive to and aware of environmental stimuli that has survival value than is normally assumed. Often this type of paranormal reception of information will manifest itself as gut feelings, hunches, avoidance behavior, thoughts, urges, and so on. It is for this reason that parapsychologists and psychics alike often urge people to become more sensitive to their subliminal responses and pay attention to them. A highly developed PMIR sensitivity obviously would be of importance to a peace officer for its survival value. In fact, there are numerous anecdotes of officers who saved their lives by paying attention to gut feelings and premonitions. It will never be known, however, how many slain officers may have had similar gut feelings or premonitions that they fatally ignored. One such instance involved a patrolman who worked with the authors on a special burglary-theft team. One night on patrol the officer had told us that he felt that a major change was coming up in his life. A few days later he spent the day straightening out his affairs at home (e.g., going through his gun collection with his wife to inform her of their value and desired disposition), said goodbye to his wife as if for the last time, and reported for duty. Later that night he was gunned down after a theft of services stop. He died almost instantly with a slug through his aorta.

PMIR is likely an instinctual survival skill and mechanism that has atrophied with the advent of civilization. Evidence for this view is the often astounding and prevalent psychic abilities of native peoples as reported by anthropologists doing fieldwork. Native peoples frequently exhibit a seemingly natural psychic survival mechanism that is triggered in some civilized people only in time of danger, if at all. This author had an experience that is still as fresh in my mind as the day it happened. I was standing on a street corner in Missoula, Montana, waiting for the traffic light to change, when suddenly I felt like someone stabbed an ice pick into my shoulder. I whirled around immediately to meet face-to-face the gaze of the most evil-looking man I'd ever seen, a Charles Manson look-alike.

One specific way PMIR may manifest itself on the job is in the form of *synchronicity*. Many investigators have witnessed certain events in a particular investigation that seemed to coincide meaningfully. We all have experienced this in our personal lives, as when we go to the phone to call a particular person and at that instant it rings and that person is on the line. After years of studying this phenomenon, Carl Jung, a famous Swiss psychiatrist and founder of the popular Jungian depth psychology, termed such meaningful coincidences synchronicity. According to Dr. Jung, they are events that are related in time and by their meaning, but there is no identifiable causal connection.

He stressed, however, that even though the existence of synchronicities cannot be explained scientifically, they nonetheless are real and important and should be taken into consideration as purposeful and meaningful.

As an example, one of the authors placed a long distance telephone call to a deputy in an adjacent state regarding using psychics to help find a missing hunter, believed to have been murdered. The author was going to recommend that the deputy call a captain in another state to verify his credentials. When the call was placed, the deputy was already "coincidentally" talking to the captain on another line, so a three-party conference call was held.

Several instances from this author's personal life illustrate how synchronicity works. My sister-in-law was approximately three weeks overdue with her first child. Family bets had been taken as to when the child would be born, and she and her husband had decided to name it Tyler if it was a boy. At exactly 4 A.M. (which is an important time in the esoteric literature, since this is the time when the body chemistry changes), I was awakened by the telephone. I answered and a man's voice asked, "Is Mr. Tyler there?" I replied that he had the wrong number and I hung up, then realizing that my nephew would be born that day, which he was.

On another occasion my brothers and I were scattering our father's ashes on the family ranch. He had been killed when his private airplane crashed. Immediately after scattering his ashes and while standing in silence, we heard an approaching aircraft. The small plane was approaching up a valley toward us, but we could not see it, because we were on the other side of the ridge. As it got closer, we all noticed that it sounded exactly like our father's plane. We waited in anticipation and finally a Super Cub like the one our father died in broke over the ridge right above us. It was the game warden, who incidentally was one of the men who found the crash site a month earlier. We all looked at each other, a little startled and impressed with the significance of what we felt to be an unspoken tribute to our father.

In another instance the authors (WH & RW) had arranged to meet with Dr. Milton Erickson of Phoenix, Arizona, to discuss his writing the foreword for our first book, *Forensic Hypnosis,* which was eventually published by Charles C Thomas, Publisher. Before leaving for Arizona, we had a conversation with a psychologist in Montana who knew Dr. Erickson. We mentioned that we were going to see him, and she replied, "If he lives long enough." A few nights later this author had a tea leaf reading done in which it was stated that things would not be as we expected when we reached Phoenix and that it had something to do with an older man. We embarked for Phoenix and spent a few days in Tucson while waiting for our appointment. On the Tuesday night before the scheduled meeting on Saturday, I became violently ill, the first time in many years. On Friday the generator on the car went out, and while we were having it fixed, a man came up to us and began talking. He proved to be the director of the largest funeral home in Arizona. After the car was fixed, we drove up to Phoenix to wait for our appointment. I called Dr. Erickson's residence to confirm the appointment, only to be told by his daughter that he had died late Tuesday night, approximately the same time as my illness. At that moment I consciously realized that at a subconscious level I had known that he had died but had failed to make the connection.

As it relates to investigation, synchronicity may be important in the following ways:

1. Examine the meaningful sequence of seemingly unrelated events, circumstances, and people that culminated in a crime.
2. Be aware of the timing of developments in the case. Does it coincide with something else, e.g., the finding of a new piece of physical evidence on the same day that you "accidentally" bump into a suspect on the street?
3. Does a television crime drama or a magazine article uncannily parallel an investigation you are working on? Watch for these kinds of parallel but seemingly unconnected events that may "comment" on your case. Are you thinking about John Doe's possible involvement when he calls and volunteers some information? Do you see your prime suspect around town several times in one day when you normally never see him?
4. Watch your dreams. Do they coincide with and tell you something about current investigations?

Synchronicities and instances of PMIR are usually not recognized as such, because they are often so ordinary. They are all too easily dismissed as mere coincidences or lucky guesses. Then there are others that strike the investigator as significant, but the meaning is not readily apparent. For instance, a detective from Idaho was investigating the disappearance and probable homicide of a young man from Missouri, who was last seen while camping in Idaho. Some of his camping equipment was impounded from two men arrested in Seattle on fraud and forgery. Several months later a body, believed to be that of the missing man, was reported found by boy scouts to a Wyoming sheriff's office just over the border from Idaho at 4:30 P.M. The missing man's sister, who had been trying to recover his property for months from Seattle, had it signed over to her at exactly the same day and time (3:30 P.M. Seattle time). The odds against such a coincidence are astronomical, yet its possible significance remains a mystery.

Another instance of synchronicity involved a sergeant in the King County Sheriff's Office in Washington State, who allegedly burned down his house for insurance proceeds on July 9, 1996. The investigation soon focused on the officer. Feeling the scrutiny of police investigators and county prosecutors, the officer decided to find a scapegoat and soon-to-be-victim. In early August, 911 received a call from a man reporting a disturbance between himself and his neighbors. The officer was on duty at the time and responded to the call, waiving off other officers. The man was last seen alive that day getting into the officer's patrol car. When the man did not call his mother as was customary in the next couple of days, she filed a missing person's report.

In early September, the officer met with an arson investigator and gave him a five-page statement, signed by the missing man. In it, the man confessed to burning down the officer's house, thus exonerating the officer. Because the person signing this confession was missing, the investigations of the arson and the missing person dovetailed. The officer became a murder suspect. Within a week, he was relieved of duty and placed on administrative leave pending the investigation.

An intense and unsuccessful search for the missing person took place over the next two months. However, an executed search warrant turned up blood in the back seat of the officer's patrol car. DNA tests matched this to the missing man's parents. The officer was booked and jailed for first-degree murder in late November 1996.

Having worked with the officer for almost eleven years, Deputy Ferenc Zana was utterly stunned by the events. When Zana read the prosecutor's probable cause statement, it became obvious to him that the officer was guilty. However, there was still no body.

It was in December 1996 that Zana came in contact with the world of "psychic spies" and remote viewing. He contacted Paul Smith, one of the original CIA-trained remote viewers, who agreed to help. Between January 29 and 31, 1997 Smith tasked three remote viewers with locating the body. On February 1, 1997, Smith faxed Zana three narratives, seven sketches, and a map with coordinates. Zana put a small team together to analyze the data. The next day the team tuned in to the six o'clock news. The lead story was that some human remains were found the day before by some hikers, which were later identified as those of the missing man.

Synchronistically, Zana realized that he and his team had just sat down in his living room to evaluate the remote viewer's information when the find was reported to the Bellevue Police Department. The hikers had found the body at the exact same time as Zana and his team began concentrating on the location of the body. Zana admits that he is "still in the twilight zone as to why the body was found after six months in the same month, on the same day, the same hour, and give or take a few minutes that I sat down to look at the psychic data." Furthermore, the RV data included an extremely accurate drawing of the area in which the body was found. "This drawing has change my life more than anything else," Zana notes, and launched his study of remote viewing.

On June 6, 1997, a six-week trial was culminated in King County Superior Court. Sergeant Matthias Bachmeier was found guilty as charged on one count of aggravated first-degree murder and sentenced to life in prison without the possibility of parole.

Ultimately the information provided by the remote viewers was "eerily accurate," according to Zana, who remains a deputy at the King County Sheriff's Office. He also has more than four year's experience with remote viewing (as a student of Lyn Buchanan) and is currently serving as Project Manager for the Assigned Witness Program.

Targ and Harary recommend that psi can be helpful in many areas of daily life, including decision making, checking out people at a distance, looking into the future, finding lost objects and missing people, avoiding mishaps and accidents, being in the right place at the right time, understanding and acting on the psi content of dreams, and generally knowing yourself and others better. Targ relates two personal stories that demonstrate the usefulness of psi. Riding his motorcycle home from the laser laboratory where he was a research scientist, he began to muse about what was around the curve ahead and wondered what he would do if there was a board in the road while traveling forty mph. He throttled back to a crawl, rounded the curve, and saw a two-by-four board lying squarely in his path. In a second incident, Targ and his wife were at a dinner party when she suddenly stood up and said that they had to go home immediately. They arrived home to find their ten-year-old son choking to death. A registered nurse, Mrs. Targ was able to avert a tragedy.

Targ and Harary believe that developing one's psychic ability is nothing special:

> Learning to be aware of your psychic abilities can be like remembering something you already know. The process involves refining and deepening your responses to subtle information, rather than tapping into foreign sources of knowledge. It is as though psychic abilities were sleeping quietly in the background of your mind, waiting for a nudge to awaken and open the lines of communication. . . . All of our research and experience strongly indicates that psychic information is readily available if you learn how to observe it.

This "nothing special," however, may save your life and help solve cases.

Chapter 8

CONCLUSION

Max Planck, the physicist who was awarded the Nobel Prize in 1918 for the formulation of the quantum theory, once observed: "A new scientific truth does not triumph by convincing its opponents and making them see the light, but rather because its opponents eventually die and a new generation grows up that's familiar with it." Such is likely to be the case with psychic criminology, which will not become an accepted investigative tool until the old command levels are replaced by new ones accustomed to the existence of psi. Such familiarity will develop at the hands of the mass media, the increasing scientific acceptance of psychic phenomena as a legitimate research concern, the eventual scientific demystification of psi, and its demonstrated practical usefulness.

In decades to come, psychic criminology likely will chart a common course, known as the "boom and bust" cycle. The first stage of the cycle is one of open skepticism and criticism, but with time and exposure the skeptics and critics realize the value of the new idea and become proponents–the second stage. The new proponents overenthusiastically embrace the technique–the third stage. When it fails to meet their unrealistically high expectations, however, they abandon it–the fourth stage. Hopefully, when psychic criminology is first widely embraced, it will be accepted and used professionally and in moderation. If unrealistic expectations are withheld and it is developed and used properly, it will take a legitimate place in the investigator's armamentarium.

It would be wise to remember, as a precautionary note, that psychic criminology will be hurt more by the excessive claims of its overzealous proponents than by the legitimate questions of its opponents. Yet it is only rational for its opponents to recognize that psychic investigation, although far from perfect, compares quite favorably with traditional police investigative procedures (which statistically are notoriously inefficient and ineffective) if developed and used properly.

Looking to the future, psychic criminology will probably follow a similar route as has psychic archaeology. In 1974, the American Anthropological Association held a special symposia on parapsychology and anthropology in Mexico City. Intense interest was demonstrated as evidenced by an attendance of approximately 400 anthropologists and archaeologists. Follow-up seminars were held in 1975, 1977, and 1978. Several professional and scholarly books and articles have been published since, and a scientific journal was begun in 1977 with the express purpose of academically exploring psychic anthropology and archaeology. After this initial enthusiasm, interest has waned to a more moderate level.

In years to come, the emerging field of psychic criminology may experience a similar development. In fact, a precedent has already been set. In the 1930s there was a meeting of the Viennese Criminological Association devoted entirely to the discussion of the use of psychic abilities and phenomena in criminal investigation, during which eminent authorities from various fields hotly debated the possibilities. Let us hope that those in authority in the United States have the foresight and open-mindedness to seriously consider and explore the use of psychics in criminology.

Appendix

INTUITIVE INVESTIGATION REPORT FORM

Type of Case —————————————— Victim ——————————

Location of Crime ————————————— Date of Crime —————————

Information Provided ——————————————————————————

————————————————————————————————————

————————————————————————————————————

————————————————————————————————————

Information Obtained ——————————————————————————

————————————————————————————————————

————————————————————————————————————

————————————————————————————————————

————————————————————————————————————

————————————————————————————————————

————————————————————————————————————

————————————————————————————————————

————————————————————————————————————

————————————————————————————————————

————————————————————————————————————

Corroboration ————————————————————————————

————————————————————————————————————

————————————————————————————————————

Investigator ——————————————— Date ————————————

GLOSSARY

Apparition. A generally spontaneous paranormal appearance of someone either distant or dead. Also known as ghosts or "ectoplasmic manifestations."

Astral Body. A hypothetical energy body that allegedly can leave the physical body.

Astral Planes. Hypothetical nonphysical levels of reality in which a person's astral body can travel.

Astral Projection. The apparent intentional or spontaneous experience of the astral body leaving the physical body. The experiencer is conscious of being out of the body. Also known as "astral travel" and "out-of-the-body experience".

Aura. The electromagnetic energy field surrounding the body that some sensitives claim to be able to see. The intensity and colors of the aura are supposed to be indicative of a person's physical, mental, and spiritual condition.

Automatic Writing. Writing performed in a dissociated state, i.e., the writer has no voluntary conscious control over what is written. The writing is believed to be performed either by the person's own unconscious mind or, in some cases, discarnate entities working through the person as a medium.

Channeling. The act of receiving or serving as a medium or "channel" for information from paranormal sources.

Entity. The energy field, soul, spirit, intelligence, or personality of a discarnate or disembodied (deceased) person. Entities may include nonhuman spirits and forces, such as nature spirits and deities.

Graphology. The science of understanding a person's character by examining his or her distinctive handwriting. A "psychographologist" is a psychic who uses handwriting samples as a vehicle or key to gaining psychic impressions of the person's deep character, tendencies, and motives not ordinarily detectable in the handwriting.

Guide. A protective and benevolent entity believed to continually watch over a person. A "guardian angel."

Hit. A correct answer or accurate information provided psychically. The opposite of a "miss."

Intuition. The spontaneous knowing of something without the conscious use of reasoning or logical inference.

Karma. The manifestation in the world of personal human affairs of the physical law: For every action there is an equal and opposite reaction. In Hinduism and

135

Buddhism it refers to the totality of one's thoughts and actions that determine one's fate or destiny in this life and succeeding incarnations; in Christianity, "as you sow, so shall you reap."

Medium. A psychic who seems to receive information directly from entities at non-trance levels or who serves as a channel for entities to communicate directly to the embodied.

Palmistry. The alleged art of "reading" a person and their condition, character, and future by the distinctive lines on the palm.

Paranormal. Psychological and physical phenomena and abilities that are beyond the "normal" as currently defined and understood by science.

Parapsychology. The branch of science that studies paranormal phenomena, such as telepathy and clairvoyance.

Possession. The apparent taking over of the mind and body of an individual by an entity.

Prana. The hypothetical life force believed to animate living matter. Also known as "ki," "chi," "odic," "orgone," and "bioplasma."

Psychokinesis (PK). The ability of a human being to affect objects, events, or other people in the absence of any direct physical contact.

Reading. The act of paranormally obtaining information. A psychic will do a "reading" to answer questions.

Reincarnation. The doctrine or belief in the rebirth after death of the spirit in another human body.

Spiritualism. A religious movement with doctrines and practices based on the belief that the dead survive as spirits and can communicate with the living, especially through a medium.

Trance. A mental condition in which one's overall mental functioning is qualitatively different from one's normal waking consciousness. Trance may be either spontaneous or induced intentionally by oneself or another. Trance has psi potential for allowing access to levels of mind and reality not ordinarily experience.

BIBLIOGRAPHY

Allison, D., & Jacobson, S.: *Dorothy Allison: A Psychic Story.* New York: Jove, 1980.

Archer, F.: *Crime and the Psychic World.* New York: Morrow, 1969.

Bartlett, L.: *Psi Trek.* New York: McGraw-Hill, 1981.

Bird, C.: *The Divining Hand: The 500-Year-Old Mystery of Dowsing.* New York: Dutton, 1979.

Brink, F.: Parapsychology and criminal investigation. *International Criminal Police Review, 134*:3-8, January 1960.

Broughton, R.: *Parapsychology: The Controversial Science.* New York: Ballantine Books, 1991.

Browne, M.: Arguing the existence of ESP. *New York Times,* January 29, 1980, pp. Cl & C3.

Browning, N.: *The Psychic World of Peter Hurkos.* New York: Doubleday, 1970.

Caldwell, C.: Beyond ESP. *New Times,* April 3, 1978, pp. 43-50.

Davis-Floyd, R., & Arvidson, P. S. (Eds.): *Intuition: The Inside Story.* New York: Routledge, 1997.

Dempsey, T.: *The Use of Psychics by Police as an Investigative Aid: An Examination of Current Trends and Potential Applications of Psi Phenomena to Law Enforcement.* Unpublished master's thesis, California State University, Long Beach, 1981.

Doran, B.: Psychic sleuths. *Student Lawyer,* November 1978, pp. 25-26.

Dykshorn, M., & Felton, R.: *My Passport Says Clairvoyant.* New York: Hawthorne, 1974.

Edge, H., Morris, R., Rush, J., & Palmer, J.: *Foundations of Parapsychology: Exploring the Boundaries of Human Capability.* New York: Routledge & Kegan Paul, 1986.

Farabee, C.: *Contemporary Psychic Use by Police in America.* Unpublished master's thesis, California State University, Fresno, 1981.

Galante, M.: Lawyers use of psychics: The wave of the future? *The National Law Journal,* January 27, 1986, pp. 1, 32-33.

Geberth, V.: Psychics. In his *Practical Homicide Investigation: Tactics, Procedures, and Forensic Techniques.* New York: Elsevier, 1983, pp. 420-424.

Gooch, S.: *The Paranormal.* New York: Harper & Row, 1978.

Goodman, J.: *Psychic Archaeology: Time Machine to the Past.* New York, Berkley, 1977.

Gordon, T., & Tobias, J.: Managing the psychic in criminal investigations. *Police Chief,* May 1979, pp. 56-59.

Guanno, R.: The police and psychics. *Psychic Magazine,* May/June, 1975.

Holzer, H.: *Psychic Investigator.* New York: Manor, 1975.

Holzer, H.: *Psychic Detective No. 1.* New York: Manor, 1976.

Hurkos, P.: *Psychic.* New York: Bobbs-Merrill, 1961.

Jaegers, B.: *The Psychic Paradigm: A Psychic Reveals the Secrets of Unlocking Your Own ESP Abilities.* New York: Berkley Putnam, 1998.

Kovach, S.: *Hidden Files: Law Enforcement's True Case Stories of the Unexplained and Paranormal.* Chicago: Contemporary Books, 1998.

Kozenczak, J., & Henrikson, K.: Still beyond belief: The use of psychics in homicide investigations. *Policing, 5*(2):131-149, 1989.

Krippner, S., & Davidson, R.: Parapsychology in the U.S.S.R. *Saturday Review,* March 18, 1972, pp. 56-60.

Leslie, D.: *Among the Zulu and the Amatongos,* 2nd ed. Privately printed, Edinburgh, 1875.

Lyons, A., & Truzzi, M.: *The Blue Sense: Psychic Detectives and Crime.* New York: The Mysterious Press, 1991.

Marshall, E.: Police science and psychics. *Science, 210:* 994-995, November 28, 1980.

Martin, D., & Levine, M.: Unlikely allies: Psychics & law enforcement agencies. *Law Enforcement Technology,* September 1990, pp. 58-60 & 63.

Mavromatis, A.: *Hypnagogia: The Unique State of Consciousness between Wakefulness and Sleep.* New York: Routledge, 1987.

McMoneagle, J.: *Mind Trek: Exploring Consciousness, Time and Space through Remote Viewing.* Charlottesville: Hampton Roads, 1993.

McMullen, G.: *One White Crow.* Norfolk: Hampton Roads, 1994.

McMurran, K.: Some days, say police, this New Jersey psychic can indeed see forever. *People.* July 16, 1979, pp. 95-101.

Mishlove, J.: *The Roots of Consciousness: Psychic Liberation through History, Science and Experience.* New York: Random House, 1975.

Mitchell, E.: *Psychic Exploration: A Challenge for Science.* New York: Putnam, 1974.

Morehouse, D.: *Psychic Warrior: Inside the CIA's Stargate Program.* New York: St. Martin's Press, 1996.

Ostrander, S., & Schroeder, L.: *Psychic Discoveries Behind the Iron Curtain.* New York: Bantam, 1970.

Parapsychology – what the questionnaire revealed. *New Scientist,* January 25, 1973, p. 209.

Pasternak, G.: Mind over murder: Psychic aids in investigation. *Law and Order,* September 1986, pp. 44-48.

Pasternak, G.: *Tour of Duty: The Diaries of Psychic Bill Ward.* 1994. Available from www.psychicdetective.com. Also available from 1st Books Publishing Library.

Police are calling on psychics for aid. *New York Times,* November 26, 1978, p. 61.

Puthoff, H., & Targ, R.: Remote viewing of natural targets. In Morris, J., Roll, W., & Morris, R. (Eds.): *Research in Parapsychology.* Metuchen, NJ: Scarecrow Press, 1975.

Rachlin, H.: Psychics and police work. *Law and Order, 41*(9):84-88, 1993.

Radin, D.: *The Conscious Universe: The Scientific Truth of Psychic Phenomena.* San Francisco: Harper*Edge,* 1997.

Reiser, M., Ludwig, L., Saxe, S., & Wagner, C.: An evaluation of the use of psychics in the investigation of major crimes. *Journal of Police Science and Administration,* 7(1):18-25, 1979.

Rhea, K., & O'Leary, M.: *The Psychic Is You.* Milibrae: Celestial Arts, 1979.

Rhine, L.: Frequency of types of experience in spontaneous precognition. *Journal of Parapsychology, 18*(2), 1954.

Rockwell, T., Rockwell, R., & Rockwell, W.: Irrational rationalists: A critique of *The Humanist's* crusade against parapsychology. *The Journal of the American Society for Psychical Research,* 72:23-34, 1978.

Rogo, D.: Psychic Sherlocks. *Human Behavior,* May 1979, p. 48.

Rudley, S.: *Psychic Detectives.* New York: Watts, 1979.

Schall, S.: Legal issues related to the use of Psi. *Archaeus, 3*:47-52, Summer 1985.

Schall, S., & Kautz, W.: Legal issues related to psi application in law enforcement. *Applied Psi, 3*:7-12, Winter 1984/85.

Schnabel, J.: *Remote Viewers: The Secret History of America's Spies.* New York: Dell, 1997.

Schwartz, S.: *The Secret Vaults of Time: Psychic Archaeology and the Quest for Man's Beginnings.* New York: Grosset & Dunlap, 1978.

Schwartz, S.: Psychic consultants provide police departments with an extra dose of the "sixth sense" every officer needs. *Intuition Magazine, 25.*

Smith, P.: *Reading the Enemy's Mind.* New York: Tor Books/Division of St. Martin's Press, 2002.

Stevenson, I.: Precognition of disasters. *Journal of the American Society for Psychical Research, 64(2),* 1970.

Sutton, R.: A look at police parapsychology. *Behind the Badge, 2*(1):95-101, 1981.

Swanson, C., Chamelin, N., & Territo, L.: *Criminal Investigation.* New York: McGraw-Hill, 1992.

Tabori, P.: *Crime and the Occult.* New York: Taplinger, 1974.

Tenhaeff, W. H. C.: The employment of paragnosts for police purposes. *Proceedings of the P. I. [Parapsychological Institute of the State University of Utrecht], 1*:15-31, December 1960.

Targ, R., & Harary, K. *The Mind Race: Understanding and Using Psychic Abilities.* New York: Villard Books, 1984.

Targ, R., & Puthoff, H.: *Mind Reach.* New York: Delacorte, 1977.

The use of psychics to aid police investigators in solving crimes. *Applied Psi Newsletter, 1*(3):1-2. July/August 1982.

Trubo, R.: Psychics and the police. *Psychic Magazine,* May/June, 1975.

Truzzi, M.: Reflections on *The Blue Sense* and its critics. *The Journal of Parapsychology, 59*:99-130, June 1995.

Use of psychics in law enforcement. *Criminal Information Bulletin* [State of California Department of Justice]. February, 1979, pp. 23-26.

Utts, J.: An assessment of the evidence for psychic functioning. *Journal of Scientific Exploration, 59*(4):3-30.

Vaughan, A.: Police: How to use psychics. *Psychic Magazine,* May/June, 1975.

White, J. (Ed.): *Frontiers of Consciousness: The Meeting Ground between Inner and Outer Reality.* New York: Julian, 1974.

Wilson, C.: *The Psychic Detectives.* London: Pan Books, 1984.

Wiseman, R.: *Deception & Self-Deception: Investigating Psychics.* Amherst, New York: Prometheus, 1997.

Wolman, B. (Ed.): *Handbook of Parapsychology.* New York: Van Nostrand Reinhold, 1977.

Woodhall, Det. Sgt. E.: *Crime and the Supernatural.* London: John Long, 1935.

Zukav, G.: *The Dancing Wu Li Masters: An Overview of the New Physics.* New York: Morrow, 1979.

INDEX

A

A Case Closed, 15
Abrahamson, Aron, 101
Accretion, 90
Allison, Dorothy, 4
American Association for Parapsychology, 47
American Institutes for Research report, 40
American Society for Psychical Research, 46, 53
  remote viewing experiments, 31
Analytical overlay, 65
Animals and fish
  extraordinary sensing abilities, 41, 124
Anomalous cognition, 39
Apparition, 139
Archeological findings, 38, 100–2 (*see also* Psychometry)
  psychic archaeology, reliability, 101–2
  psychometry, 38–39, 100–2
  success factors, 101
  testing grounds for psychic abilities, 100
  triple-blind test, 100
Army Research Institute report, 40
Assigned Witness Program, 17, 58, 129
Astral body, 139
Astral plane, 139
Astral projection, 139
Astral writing, 18, 35, 139
Aura, 77, 139
  correlation with polygraph, 77
Automatic writing, 18, 139
Avoidance behavior, 125

B

Barber, T. X., 41, 42
Basil, James, 8
Belle, Judy, 16
Bias
  block to new information, 42–43
Blue sense, 45
Books and periodicals
  American Psychologist (accepting articles), 47
  Behavioral and Brain Sciences (accepting articles), 47
  Blue Sense: Psychic Detectives and Crime, vii, 11
  Criminal Investigation, 100
  Deception & Self-Deception: Investigating Psychics, 100
  European Journal of Parapsychology, 47
  Foundations of Parapsychology, 44
  Foundations of Physics (accepting articles), 47
  Journal for the Society for Psychical Research, 47
  Journal of Parapsychology, 47
  Journal of Police Science and Administration (accepting articles), 20
  Journal of the American Society for Psychical Research, 47
  Mind Race, 31
  National Law Review (accepting articles), 20
  New Scientist, 46
  Physical Review (accepting articles), 47
  Police Chief (accepting articles), 20, 21
  Policing (accepting articles), 20
  Practical Homicide Investigation (accepting

141

Charles C Thomas
PUBLISHER • LTD.

P.O. Box 19265
Springfield, IL 62794-9265

- Schafer, John R. & Joe Navarro—**ADVANCED INTERVIEWING TECHNIQUES: Proven Strategies for Law Enforcement, Military, and Security Personnel.** '04, 118 pp. (7 x 10).

- O'Hara, Charles E. & Gregory L. O'Hara—**FUNDAMENTALS OF CRIMINAL INVESTIGATION.** (7th Ed.) '03, 928 pp. (6 x 9), 76 il., $59.95, cloth.

- O'Hara, Gregory L.—**A REVIEW GUIDE FOR FUNDAMENTALS OF CRIMINAL INVESTIGATION.** (**7th Ed.**) '03, 310 pp. (7 x 10), $33.95, paper.

- Covey, Herbert C.—**STREET GANGS THROUGHOUT THE WORLD.** '03, 280 pp. (7 x 10), 1 table, $59.95, hard, $39.95, paper.

- Nicholson, William C.—**EMERGENCY RESPONSE AND EMERGENCY MANAGEMENT LAW: Cases and Materials.** '03, 366 pp. (7 x 10), 21 il., $79.95, hard, $54.95, paper.

- Flowers, R. Barri—**MALE CRIME AND DEVIANCE: Exploring Its Causes, Dynamics, and Nature.** '03, 370 pp. (7 x 10), 33 il., 41 tables, $70.95, hard, $49.95, paper.

- Payne, Brian K.—**CRIME IN THE HOME HEALTH CARE FIELD: Workplace Violence, Fraud, and Abuse.** '03, 192 pp. (7 x 10), 17 il., 11 tables, $46.95, hard, $29.95, paper.

- Payne, Brian K.—**INCARCERATING WHITE-COLLAR OFFENDERS: The Prison Experience and Beyond.** '03, 192 pp. (7 x 10), 12 il., 20 tables, $47.95, hard, $30.95, paper.

- Garner, Gerald W.—**COMMON SENSE POLICE SUPERVISION: Practical Tips for the First-Line Supervisor. (3rd Ed.)** '03, 318 pp. (7 x 10), $68.95, hard, $48.95, paper.

- Castellano-Hoyt, Don W.—**ENHANCING POLICE RESPONSE TO PERSONS IN MENTAL HEALTH CRISIS: Providing Strategies, Communication Techniques, and Crisis Intervention Preparation in Overcoming Institutional Chal-lenges.** '03, 314 pp. (7 x 10), $66.95, hard, $46.95, paper.

- Bannon, Mark E.—**A Quick Reference Guide To Contemporary CRIMINAL PROCEDURE For Law Enforcement Officers: One Hundred Notable United States Supreme Court Decisions, and Their Effect on Modern Policing in America.** '03, 174 pp. (7 x 10), $43.95, hard, $27.95, paper.

- Passamaneck, Stephen M.—**POLICE ETHICS AND THE JEWISH TRADITION.** '03, 188 pp. (7 x 10), $49.95, hard, $34.95, paper.

- Smith, Jim—**A LAW ENFORCEMENT AND SECURITY OFFICERS' GUIDE TO RESPONDING TO BOMB THREATS: Providing a Working Knowledge of Bombs, Preparing for Such Incidents, and Performing Basic Analysis of Potential Threats.** '03, 172 pp. (7 x 10), 11 il., $41.95, hard, $25.95, paper.

- O'Reilly, James T.—**POLICE TRAFFIC STOPS AND RACIAL PROFILING: Resolving Management, Labor and Civil Rights Conflicts.** '02, 304 pp. (7 x 10), $65.95, hard, $46.95, paper.

- Fredrickson, Darin D. & Raymond P. Siljander—**RACIAL PROFILING: Eliminating the Con-fusion Between Racial and Criminal Profiling and Clarifying What Constitutes Unfair Discrimination and Persecution.** '02, 170 pp. (7 x 10), $43.95, hard, $27.95, paper.

- Holmes, Warren D.—**CRIMINAL INTERROGATION: A Modern Format for Interrogating Criminal Suspects Based on the Intellectual Approach.** '02, 166 pp. (7 x 10), $42.95, hard, $27.95, paper.

- Kelly, Jan Seaman—**FORENSIC EXAMINATION OF RUBBER STAMPS: A Practical Guide.** '02, 242 pp. (8 1/2 x 11), 345 il., $61.95, hard, $40.95, paper.

- Coppock, Craig A.—**CONTRAST: An Investiga-tor's Basic Reference Guide to Fingerprint Identification Concepts.** '01 148 pp. (7 x 10), 65 il., $39.95, hard, $25.95, paper.

- Mijares, Tomas C., Ronald M. McCarthy, & David B. Perkins—**THE MANAGEMENT OF POLICE SPECIALIZED TACTICAL UNITS.** '00, 218 pp. (7 x 10), 3 tables, $49.95, cloth, $32.95, paper.

5 easy ways to order!

PHONE:
1-800-258-8980
or (217) 789-8980

FAX:
(217) 789-9130

EMAIL:
books@ccthomas.com
Web: www.ccthomas.com

MAIL:
Charles C Thomas •
Publisher, Ltd.
P.O. Box 19265
Springfield, IL 62794-9265

Complete catalog available at ccthomas.com • books@ccthomas.com

Books sent on approval • Shipping charges: $6.95 min. U.S. / Outside U.S., actual shipping fees will be charged • Prices subject to change without notice